SERVING THE CH

The Good Parish Management Guide

Other titles in the *Serving the Church* series:

A Lay Eucharistic Minister's Handbook Ann Tomalak

A Handbook for Children's Liturgy Barbara Mary Hopper

SERVING THE CHURCH

Series Editors: Michael and Kathleen Walsh

The Good Parish Management Guide

How to revive your parish

Ian Smith

CANTERBURY
PRESS
Norwich

First published in 2006 by the Canterbury Press Norwich
(a publishing imprint of Hymns Ancient & Modern Limited, a
registered charity)
9–17 St Albans Place, London N1 0NX

www.scm-canterburypress.co.uk

British Library Cataloguing in Publication data

A catalogue record for this book is available
from the British Library

ISBN 1-85311-672-6
978-1-85311-672-8

Typeset by Regent Typesetting, London
Printed and bound in Great Britain by
William Clowes Ltd, Beccles, Suffolk

Contents

To
Alison, Kirsty, Dominique and Rosalind.

Thank you!

Series Introduction

This is one of a series of handbooks designed to help lay people play a greater part in the life of the Church. It is usual nowadays to find lay men and women reading at Mass, administering Communion, organizing children's liturgy, even sometimes leading eucharistic services in the absence of a priest. Lay people commonly organize the music for Mass and other liturgical events in the parish. Many are asked to help out in other ways, sometimes even outside the boundaries of the parish, by becoming, for example, governors of the local Catholic school. For all these tasks, and other roles that the laity now play, the authors of the books in this series have tried to describe what is entailed in the particular role or ministry to which you have been called. They have provided something of the history and the theology where appropriate. They understand that people are willing, but often need encouragement to take on tasks that, in the past, may have seemed the special preserve of the clergy.

They also understand that those approached to undertake these ministries are often busy people with jobs to do and families to care for. The books are therefore as concise as it is possible to make them, written in straightforward language with a minimum of technical jargon (though glossaries are supplied where necessary) and include a good deal of practical advice.

We hope that these books will be helpful, not just in the practical details of fulfilling a ministry within the Church, but also in developing a deeper, more spiritual understanding of the mysteries of the Catholic faith.

Kathleen and Michael Walsh

Introduction

Building the Kingdom of God on Earth

'... whoever wants to become great among you must be your servant, and whoever wants to be first must be your slave.'

Matthew 20.26–27

There is no doubt that this book has ambitions.

Its first ambition is that it will contribute to people's ability to manage their parishes more effectively. It aims to use sound management principles but it wants to base the approach on Christ's teachings. If we could end up being Christ-centred managers, then this book will have succeeded in its first ambition.

Its next ambition is to open up this management to the whole parish. Of course, the book is aimed at those who will be expected to take on management roles within the parish, but it demonstrates that in parishes no one can or should try to do everything. It also reveals that in our parishes, we all take on some measure of responsibility and that we are all expected to help make the parish work. So, we all end up sharing in management of the parish. If we can understand what is going on, if we can appreciate the problems and if we can do our small part more effectively, we will all be contributing to a better managed parish.

So, the book's second ambition is to be relevant and useful to everyone who takes their parish seriously. If we are the parish, we have to be the parish.

The book's third ambition is to help every parish to start building the kingdom of God here on earth. It is not intending to provide worship and other such materials. It simply recognizes that the more we work together, the better we build our communities in our parishes, and the more we strive to live out our faith, the closer we will get to this ambition. So, making it easier to work together and sharing the load will be part of it. So will caring and loving for one another, understanding each other and showing each other true respect.

The book's final ambition is that it wants the reader to discover some of the principles of Christ-centred management. It wants the reader to apply these principles in every area of parish life. The book cannot cover every aspect and so it does not even try to do this. The world changes; rules, laws and circumstances change; but Christ's teachings endure. If we base our management behaviour on this, we should reach our goal in the best manner possible. In the end, the book is not so much about what we have to get done but how we go about doing it.

So, welcome to your parish. Discover that what you have is precious. Let us all see what we can build from such worthy foundations.

1
What is a Parish?

'Again, I tell you that if two of you on earth agree about anything you ask for, it will be done for you by my Father in heaven. For where two or three come together in my name, there am I with them.'

Matthew 18.19–20

Introduction

Almost by default, readers of this book can be expected to have some idea of what a parish is. Knowing what a parish is in technical terms is like knowing what a person is. Each is readily identified as being a parish (or person) but every one is different.

The origin of the parish

The origins of the *parish* lie in the early Church. They were built around the necessities of sharing and worshipping together. Its structure grew out of the first-century synagogue. Just like the synagogues, the early churches were led by one or more presbyters, or elders (the origin of the word as well as the role of the priest). When a community ended up with a number of these presbyters, it elected a leader, or *episkopos*, which can be translated as 'supervisor' and is the origin of the English word 'bishop'. For quite a long time these bishops performed their supervisory functions by doing circuits of the churches they were responsible for. Deacons also appear in the early period of church development. They may have performed some administrative role but they were also key players in worship and sacramental life, and there are some fascinating records regarding their role in Baptism (see John Wijngaards, 2002). So, the early Church saw its congregations being served by deacons, priests and bishops in a system which was growing in hierarchical terms as the whole Church expanded. The building-block for Christian communities became what we generally describe as the parish.

The idea of a parish, then, has its roots deeply embedded in the early Church, and the word has as its origins the Latin word *parochia* and its related Greek word *paroikia*, meaning an ecclesiastical district. The root words *para*, meaning 'beside', and *oikos*, meaning 'a dwelling', give added emphasis to what a parish was and basically still is. It denotes the neighbourhood or catchment area around a church where the people are served by the priest or minister attached to that church. It is also a lot more than that: the parish is also bound up with what 'church' is.

The English-speaking world uses the word 'church' in a variety of contexts, mixing the concept of the building within which people worship, the people who are the worshippers and the institution(s) themselves. The universal or catholic Church, whether it is referring to the Roman Catholic Church or the whole Church as recognized by a range of different churches tends to have a capital 'C'. This word's origins are in the Greek word *Kurios* meaning 'master' or 'lord' and it referred to people belonging to the Lord. Its origins are in the idea of the place or building where the people of the Lord gather and is a concept that comes later than the other word used for 'church' by most other European languages. The early Church talked about itself as a people, not a building, and, for example, the French for 'church' reflects this as *église*. This comes from the Greek *ekklesia* which means 'called out' (the French derivative can be translated as a gathering or assembly of people).

The concept of parish that we will be talking about should be understood in the following ways.

First, it is the people who worship and share God's community within an area which has a church at its centre.

Next, it is the institutional and physical aspects which come together to serve that community and operate within the requirements, rules and guidelines of the church to which it belongs.

Then it is the wider community which is served by and can be evangelized by the church or community we have defined.

It includes all the activities and processes as well as all of the physical aspects of the parish, but while its physical locus might be the church building, its core must be the people who are in some way members of Christ's community; in other words, the congregation.

Looking at some details

The primary characteristic of a parish is that it is a community of Christian people who worship together and share the same faith and denomination within that faith. The parish may also be defined such that all the people who live within the designated community are regarded as also being actual or potential members of that parish. The members of the parish may regard it as part of their calling to serve the whole community and also seek to convert them either directly or by some other means.

The geographical aspect is quite common, although there are parishes serving groups on national or ethnic lines which allow them to come together to worship in a common language.

Another common characteristic is the idea of the parish being centred on a building where worship can take place.

The other common factor is the idea that the parish is served by a specific pastor/vicar/priest whose duty is to the members of the parish or the community defined by the parish boundaries. In this modern world we find that not all parishes are served by such a person, and in a number of circumstances we will find that a number of parishes may share the services of a single person.

Parishes are expected to be subdivisions of a diocese (in the case of Anglican and Catholic churches, at least) and are organized in order to make administrative and co-operative management possible. In other words, they are populations of worshippers who, by being brought together, can operate together as a group and can both be recognized by the rest of their denomination and society at large and can manage their affairs effectively, too.

Parishes mainly consist of those who live within or, sometimes, work within the defined definitions of what the parish boundaries are.

However, parishioners may also include those who, for one reason or another, simply regard themselves as being part of that parish. Common examples of this include those whose children attend a school served by a particular church, resulting in the family becoming part of that parish despite having a parish much closer to their home. Or it may include those who decide that the parish they live in does not serve their needs, resulting in them attaching themselves to an alternative parish elsewhere.

In addition to the general definitions of what a parish is, we should also consider that the population and character of a parish also define it. Thus, we can look at its size both geographically and by population characteristics. Some parishes may cover quite large areas of land but consist of only a very small number of people. In contrast, other parishes may be small geographically yet hold a considerable number of people. Typically, the scale from very rural to inner city can be defined by this, but variations within this can also be quite significant.

The location of the parish may have other implications, including the *demographic* nature of the population (this includes the population's age, gender mix and so on), *social* characteristics (including their class, educational and family aspects), *economic* factors (such as income, employment status, home ownership and so on) and *national/ethnic* characteristics. The dominant factors in any community will help define the needs, desires and behaviour of that community, and parishes are defined as much by these factors as they are by size or geography. So, a predominantly old, middle-class, rural parish might be expected to be quite different from a young, ethnically mixed and very working-class, inner-city parish.

Furthermore, the nature of dominant individuals or groups within a parish may also have a profound effect on the parish as a whole and how it can be defined. Thus, a dominant pastor or priest is likely to define much of what the parish is like and how it is operating. This may result in there being a very dynamic, growing parish or one that is rapidly diminishing as parishioners 'vote with their feet'. Alternatively, the influencing force might be that of another 'official' or by a group such as a parish team or even a school attached to the parish. Thus, it appears that an individual or small number of people can determine the outlook and behaviour of the parish and therefore its dominant characteristics.

The nature of the community a parish sits within can have a profound effect on how it operates. For example, if the members of the parish are significantly different from the dominant population of the area, the parish may find itself acting defensively because of those differences or because their difference flags them as a target for discrimination and even attack. This may result in the parish behaving in ways that are atypical or completely at odds with the behaviour one would normally expect of them. The effects can be positive or negative. For example, the parish may develop a strong affinity with inter-faith groups in the area, be deeply involved in the local Churches Together bodies, be committed to social action or be galvanized into being an active evangelizing parish.

The life of the parish

Parishes are living things. They have a spiritual core and how this is expressed helps us understand them better. This can be seen in the life of the parish which is expressed in both spiritual and human community terms.

This life of the parish can be seen:

- *Through each day*. The activities of each church and parish will be dictated by the spiritual life it supports. Provisions for worship will vary between denominations, but private and community-based prayer and worship will take place on a daily basis.
- *Through the weeks*. For example, in some Anglican parishes, Eucharistic services may happen once a month because that is what the parish prefers or because limited access to suitable clergy dictates it. Parishes may also have themes or other patterns which reoccur across the weeks (monthly youth services, fortnightly Latin Masses, quarterly healing services and so on).
- *Through the seasons*. Each denomination has its own approach to the seasons, with common seasonal factors dominating all Christian

calendars: Advent and Christmas, Easter, Lent, and so on. As with the other patterns of life, the character of the parish will help define how the seasons are answered and revealed through the worship and spiritual life lived there.

- *Through the years.* In addition to the yearly cycles, we can see other patterns across the years. So, the AGM is annual but election of certain officers may be every three years. The parish may plan to have a mission or similar event at set intervals of a number of years duration, and so on.

The way that the parish manages to serve and express the spiritual life of its parishioners illustrates its current vitality and potential. This book will help you explore this further.

Alongside the patterns identified above, consider the following:

- *The way the parish reaches outwards and inwards.* The parish may provide its parishioners with education, evangelism, ecumenical leadership and inter-faith dialogue. In each case the flow is both inwards and outwards. With *education* it can teach to the converted and to the curious. Through *evangelism* it can help renew the faith of its parishioners while offering access to Life in Jesus. Through *ecumenical leadership* it can build bridges of understanding and support across parishes and denominations, thus supporting and deepening faith generally. Finally, *inter-faith dialogue* can support and define faith while promoting mutual respect and understanding.
- *How the parish enables its parishioners to express their faith.* The parish can help parishioners respond to the needs of the community and the wider world. It can do this through direct action and with simple responses such as allowing parish premises to be used for meetings, mother and toddler groups, advice sessions, and so on.
- *How the parish serves the community as a whole.* In addition to the provisions described above, the parish can offer itself as a focal point for public meetings and functions, thus providing resources that enrich the life of the community as a whole. The parish may also be involved in any local plans preparing for the aftermath of a local disaster or major incident of any kind.

Other parish models

These include:

- *New parish groups within church.* Rather than changing the nature of existing services which serve the current parish population, a new service is introduced and a new group (growing numbers of young people or distinctive ethnic populations for example) begins to have its needs met.
- *New parish group in a church plant.* Classic examples are where a parish does work in a new housing development and opens a small daughter church somewhere on the estate, often using community buildings; or where part of the parish experiences rapid growth and the parish plants a new congregation there.
- *New partnership initiatives.* For example, a new ethnic or other group becomes big enough to be served and the parish provides a home for their worship.
- *Sharing a worship centre.* Where different denominations and in some cases even different faith groups get together and occupy a large site. The various groups then use the centre in their own appropriate ways. From time to time large joint, ecumenical or other services may also take place.
- *House churches.* These can form a 'distributed parish' with small groups praying and worshipping together in people's houses across the parish and served by one or more priest or pastor. They may not have any centre or church and only come together a small number of times each year.
- *Parishes with cells.* These cells are not house churches but are based on the 'organic' idea of a cell structure. Small groups of eight to ten people come together for regular worship, exploration of faith and other topics. This is done in addition to and in order to enhance the parish's faith life. As these cells grow they will split in two and both cells then continue to grow until they, in turn, split and grow. Thus, the cells form a source of spiritual growth and renewal within the parish.
- *Satellite and centre churches.* Similar to house churches, this can be the way in which the parish experiences regular, weekly or more

frequent worship in small, house-based groups with less regular gatherings of the whole congregation coming together for extended services (say once a month).

Of course, there are many varieties and combinations of types of parish possible, and these are simply listed to help encourage the reader to examine their own parish and discover its pattern and nature.

Hierarchical contexts

Parishes do not exist in isolation. Their relationship with other parishes, and with the hierarchical structure within their mother church, will also help define their distinctive nature. So the reader might wish to consider the following when looking at this aspect of their parish:

- *How close to the diocese/archdiocese?* This may be determined by a number of factors such as by the person who is priest or vicar in the parish or by some other factor such as the position of an officer of the parish, or by some of its members, or simply by its geography or history.
- *How close to the deanery centre or parish?* The deanery may be different from the diocese and the diocesan centre. In addition to a different level of co-operation the parish may enjoy a greater say at this level.
- *How close to the sub-deanery level?* Similar to the case at deanery level, more autonomy and closer ties may affect a parish.
- *How does it relate to other parishes?* This may be a question which is dominated by the decline in clergy numbers and subsequent linking up of parishes. Alternatively it may be a question of how active or passive the parish is or where it is geographically.

Elements of all or some of these will be found in each parish.

Parishes: the sum of their parts

We have begun to realize that parishes can be as varied and change-able as the societies they serve. They may reflect these communities but they also reflect the denominations they are part of. Or, rather, as the essential fabric of the church bodies they belong to, parishes also reflect the structures and laws of those church bodies.

In the Catholic Church, priests are the centres of authority and responsibility in their parish. They are free to form or discontinue any parish body, can appoint and dismiss members and can decide policy and direction accordingly. In practice, priests tend to recognize the need to maintain a harmonious community and many are aware that the parish does not revolve entirely around them. Apart from the Parish Finance Committee, the priest does not need to form any parish group, but in practice he will agree to the formation of many different groups in his parish.

Many Catholic parishes have been very slow to employ paid staff. This is due to the historical reliance on clergy and professed religious and because the church has preferred to use unpaid volunteers. Indeed, there has been a tendency in the church to frown upon paying for what has been regarded as voluntary work.

The Catholic priest's most common paid staff member is now the parish secretary. Many other key roles are unpaid but parishes can employ people as parish assistants, youth workers and so on. A small number of parishes have more than one priest. This is mainly when a newly ordained priest spends a few years working as an assistant priest, learning the detailed and day-to-day aspects of his vocation.

The Anglican Church has more people built into its formal struc-tures. Each parish has (or plans to have) its incumbent, or parish priest (or rector, vicar or priest-in-charge). She or he might have a single or a group of churches, depending on the nature of the parish; and they may have one or more assistant curates (or simply curates) helping them.

Each parish usually has two churchwardens and the Parochial Church Council (PCC). The people in these roles are given real power and have legal responsibilities placed in their hands rather than in the priest's. *Churchwardens* form direct links between the parish and the bishop and between the parish priest and the congregation. They are expected to encourage the parish in their faith and practice while acting to keep the community peaceful and harmonious. They are important members of the PCC (and its standing committee) and have a duty to ensure that the PCC carries out its key duties. They take responsibility for the allocation of seating during services and maintain the peace within the church. Their duties extend to the maintenance of the church building, and are required to arrange annual inspections of buildings and report them to the parish. Churchwardens are chosen by the parishioners at an annual meeting organized for that purpose.

The *PCC* is also elected by the parish at a special meeting known as the Annual Parochial Church Meeting (APCM). This body has a full list of responsibilities which include controlling the finances and maintenance of all the parish buildings, etc. They also work with the parish priest to do her or his work, and its members represent the parish at deanery and other meetings. They also carry out a number of duties in relation to appointing and employing parish officers and staff such as a verger, administrator and the organist or musical director.

Again, much of the life of the parish will revolve around groups and activities led and run by parishioners.

The mosaic of parish life creates a picture reflecting local history, social, cultural and economic make-up, geography and the strengths of individuals within the parish. Interestingly, most are recognizable as parishes regardless of how different they are from the 'norm'.

Conclusions

The definition of what a parish is cannot be easily covered using simple dictionary definitions. In order to be able to improve our management of our parish we need to begin to look closely at how our parish works and then build on what we find. Once we have learned more about our parish, we can use good principles and practices to help us develop its management.

2
The Organization Known as the Parish

*And I pray that you, being rooted and established in love, may have power,
together with all the saints, to grasp how wide and long and high and deep is the
love of Christ.*

Ephesians 3.17–18

How is the parish put together?

We have already considered the parish in a number of general and historical ways. It is now time to look more closely at your own parish.

The elements making up a parish will vary from place to place, and
there can be no exhaustive list for all parishes. As part of this exploration
we suggest that you try listing all of the different elements you believe to
make up the parish as a whole. Think of the different services and who
they are for and who attends them; think of the different groups linked
with the parish, who are the individuals and groups who work to serve the
parish, how is the parish linked with the community and with the greater
church and other denominations in the local area, and so on. Against each
element try to say how many people are involved (in running and in being
served, etc.) and how they link up with the church (central to the parish
spiritual life, community, social life, Christian support/welfare, and so
on).

Once you have completed your list, run through the items outlined
below and compare the two lists. Change your list accordingly and
keep it as a basic list for reference later. You may find yourself adding
to this list several times during and after reading this book.

The spiritual-based elements

- *The priest(s)/vicars/assistant priests or curates/deacons/worship leaders.* Who are the people at the very core of the parish's spiritual activities? Who leads worship and leads or facilitates the main elements of spiritual life within the parish?
- *Those with other key spiritual roles.* Who are the individuals and groups with responsibility for elements within worship, rites and liturgies? These may include readers or lectors, special ministers, acolytes, MCs, churchwardens, musicians, and so on: in other words, all who take on particular roles directly related to the worship in ordinary and special services.
- *Those with support roles during services of all kinds.* This may include all those whose roles enable any particular service to happen, and although their role may have a spiritual aspect, it is basically functional, practical. It may include those who hand out and receive hymn books and Bibles, ushers, technical support people such as sound and lighting engineers, etc.
- *Other spiritual groups and individuals serving the parish.* The spiritual life of the parish may include a number of other facets, i.e. cell or house prayer groups, Bible study groups, Alpha or similar groups, RCIA (Rite of Christian Initiation for Adults) and similar groups, specific prayer or worship groups (including Catholic Rosary groups, healing and praise groups, etc.), instruction groups for baptism, First Communion, Confirmation, marriage, and so on.
- *Other spiritual activities related to groups linked with the parish.* These may include groups not wholly spiritual in function but who may also come together to worship or pray together. This may include mother and toddler groups, business and working people's clubs, youth and children's groups (including Cubs, Scouts, Guides, etc.), charity-based groups, seasonal groups (including Advent and Lenten groups), social clubs and similar groups. These groups may have annual or more regular services for members and supporters.
- *Inter-church and inter-faith groups.* These include those serving on Churches Together, inter-faith committees or similar.
- *Other spiritual-based groups and individuals.* Who else has not been

mentioned? What other elements can be added to the list that do not come under the earlier headings?

Church-based elements

The parish can expect to have a set of links with its church and related organizations. Some of these may also be mentioned in other categories but we need to consider what elements of the parish have direct links with the parent church.

- *Individuals*. Various parish members will have either statutory or other important links with the diocese. In addition to your priest or vicar, the deacons, churchwardens and key officers of the Parish Council should be regularly working with parts of the diocese structure. Other people may include a parish surveyor or architect, officers of particular groups, specially appointed parish representatives at deanery and diocesan levels, and so on.
- *Groups*. In addition to individuals, there will be groups with direct links to the diocese and deanery, to diocesan and national organizations, specialist role departments (education, legal, child protection, disability advice departments, etc.).
- *Special links*. Where parishes are sharing priests or vicars, some other spiritual and pastoral roles may also be shared or devolved to lay members or part-time ministers. Usually, there is a combination which suits both the needs of each parish while fitting the resources available.

Community-based elements

- *Those serving the parish directly*. All those with a pastoral role such as the officers of the parish, including the Parish Council, those involved in the upkeep and maintenance of the parish buildings, the financial and administrative people, the groups and committees set up to ensure that all of the physical and social aspects of the parish run smoothly, cleaning, flower arranging, and so on.

- *Those linking the parish with other elements within the local community.* This may include the inter-faith and inter-denomination groups, but also links with local schools, libraries, police, community groups, welfare and other groups, hospitals, parks and gardens, local businesses and charities, sport and social activities, civic and other functions, cemeteries and other aspects which could be spiritual but are not always approached as such. Some of these groups will provide practical support and direct involvement, and others will provide fundraising and other support.
- *Those elements of the community that touch the parish.* Any groups using your parish facilities such as other denominations or religious groups, political and social groups (including sports groups such as badminton players, keep fit, etc.), other groups with special needs (such as Alcoholics Anonymous), occasional users such as schools and clubs, and those groups who wish to hold public or social functions.

How do these elements fit with our understanding of what a parish is? If we summarize the main elements answering the question, 'What does *every* parish serve?', we come to a very familiar list of headings.

Figure 2.1 lists these under four general headings as shown. Under each heading are the most commonly agreed elements. How does your parish do compared with this? What are you covering well, and what is missing?

Is the parish one or more communities?

We keep referring to the parish as a single, amorphous mass of people. Clearly it is much more complex. We have already looked at how the parish serves a wide range of individuals and groups and how different groups within the parish are serving the parish. Let's look at this in more detail.

Figure 2.1. The aspects served by all parishes.

The parish serves . . .

God

Through:	• worship
	• living as commanded
	• serving others
	• serving one another
	• evangelization

The Church

Through:	• serving God
	• being a Christian community
	• contributing to the Church as a whole
	• acting as the Church in the community
	• being living witnesses to Christ

The world

By:	• giving access to salvation
	• teaching
	• evangelization
	• giving love and support
	• being a voice in the world
	• being a beacon

The parish community

Through providing:	• the physical resources
	• spiritual teaching
	• spiritual guidance
	• the Sacraments
	• a focus to bring the community together
	• support and love

Figure 2.2. Forces affecting the shape of worship life.

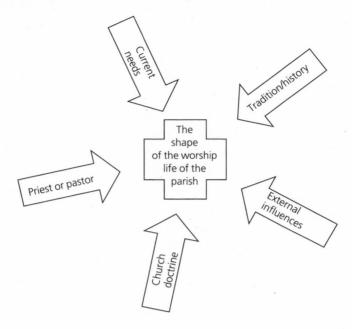

Worshipping communities

Each parish is centred on its worship life. However, parishes may have quite different approaches to and patterns of daily and weekly worship. The differences come from a number of obvious influences (see Figure 2.2). The priest or pastor will help determine worship life within the parish, depending on their needs, abilities and spiritual motivations and inspirations. Current church doctrine will also help shape things, as will the traditions and historically established activities of the parish. Then we have the current needs of different groups within the parish. Finally, there will be a number of external and other influences which help shape and drive the worship life of each parish.

So, a parish containing a dominant non-British or non-Christian population will be different from one with a largely older, more traditional upper-middle-class population. Naturally, the expected outcomes from these situations can be quite the reverse of the realities. For example, the first might result in a very old-fashioned, traditional approach to worship while the second results in a vibrant, modern, evangelical, charismatic approach.

Even within parishes with a distinct approach or character we will find more than one community being catered for. So, while the most obvious and busiest service on Sunday is predominantly modern music and very lively, we will find other services on Sunday and often during the rest of the week serving the needs of a quieter, more conservative or contemplative group of people. Conversely, there may be more lively and challenging worship located in small groups, house groups or cells dotted throughout the parish.

When reviewing your parish's worship life there are two simple approaches you can adopt. The first is to try to work out (either yourself or with a group of parishioners and your priest) what is going on in your parish.

A simple table like the one shown in Figure 2.3 will help. Start with the activities in the church or worship centre and work out from there. Try to cover every activity.

Figure 2.3. Table of worship life in the parish.

Forms of worship/ prayer/liturgy in the parish	Times	Locations	Approximate numbers involved	What do we know about those involved?

This exercise will help bring into focus the richness and diversity of your parish and help you understand the focus and boundaries of worship within your community. Use it to start discussions on parish resources and to build on existing strengths or deal with any problems or weaknesses. It will also be a good opportunity to focus your prayer and support for the different groups within the parish, opening up potential channels of dialogue and exchange.

In addition to any review/listing exercise, you might want to consider carrying out a survey to find out more about your parish. Surveys often arise from the discussion and re-examination process that follows the listing exercise. In the survey you can explore both what is good and what is missing from the parish and place it alongside the needs and aspirations of the parish as a whole. You can look at the background, motivations and inspirations of those involved in different aspects of the parish's spiritual life and explore what they do both within and outside the parish to satisfy these elements of their life. You can begin to build a picture of what the parish is like and what it might become. How much you put into the survey and how far you wish to go are up to you and your fellow parishioners. More details on this kind of approach appear in later chapters.

Before carrying out a survey, review the information you already have and see if you can form a clear picture of your parish. How can you define the general nature of your parish community, and is there a model you can use to make sense of what you find?

Some aspects to consider when doing this are:

- Is your parish church focused or quite dispersed in terms of its worship?
- Does your parish serve a wide range of different groups or communities and their needs or does it focus on a single core group's needs?
- Does it rely solely on the priest or vicar for all of its worship/prayer/ praise activities or are they shared within the community?
- Is the nature of your worship similar and focused across all groups or does the nature of the worship and prayer vary widely from group to group (they may all be acceptable and valid approaches approved

by the church but different in terms of their character, such as being more or less formal, using different types of music or language, etc.)?

Once you begin to ask these questions you will start to see how your parish is shaped and how you might begin to discuss its nature and future.

Communities that serve

Parishes exist to serve the family of God that lives, shares and worships together within the parish boundaries. It is also there to serve the greater population of the parish. The parish also serves the community through working with other faith communities and with the authorities to bring life and richness to the community as a whole.

There are differences between the Church of England and the Catholic Church with regard to what this means and how this is carried out, but the principles are basically the same. The Church of England, being the established church of the nation, has a legal as well as a moral duty to act for the whole community. Links at Churches Together level and in the various councils established between different churches (Clergy Fraternal, for example) and different faiths (inter-faith councils) help bring parishes and churches together to serve their local communities.

How does your parish serve the community?

Figure 2.4 can be used to explore outward-looking groups further. This can be done individually but it is better to work on this with others. Together you can employ the use of flip-charts, work in small teams or as a larger group.

Figure 2.4. Example of chart exploring external communities served.

External group and how served	How the parish serves	Who is involved	Links with the parish	Purposes in providing service
Mothers and their toddlers served by the Mothers & Toddlers Group.	Provide space. Provide equipment. Some of the parishioners help run it. Parish financially subsidizes it.	Parish Hall Committee. M&T Group Management Team. Individual parishioners as helpers and users.	Less than half of users are parishioners. Historical provision. Regular source of new parishioners (without evangelizing activities).	Service needed. Limited places to hold such service. Alternatives expensive. Provided through neighbourly love.

From this you will be able to gauge the level of commitment your parish has to its local community. The exercise may cause you to wonder whether the parish is doing too little, enough or too much. We will look at how you might develop that debate later. Here, we want to look at how this fits into our understanding of the parish as it exists today.

Who is responsible for what, and how is the parish currently run?

As you progress through the book you will build your own view of the basic nature of your parish's management style. Here we want to look at how the parish fits together.

Figure 2.5 is a chart in which we want to map responsibility and authority, and we will do it in a simple and direct way. The things we are seeking will tell us where the flow of responsibility goes to, who is providing the managerial and other types of support, and who is doing the practical work.

Figure 2.5. Example of an activities chart.

(a) Activities	(b) Direct responsibility	(c) Managed by	(d) Reports to	(e) Funded by

In column (a) we list each of the different types of activity we have found in the parish. This will be a long list, so we might want to subdivide it into 'Worship', and 'Serving the parish', 'Serving the community' or some other division which suits your parish best. Column (b) lists the person or people who are involved in making that activity happen. You might want to list them as teams with titles if there are too many in some of the activities. Column (c) lists the people who take on direct responsibility for keeping the activity going and co-ordinating the efforts of those taking part or running it. This may also be a team or committee. Column (d) is the person or people that those listed in (c) report to. If it is the parish, ask yourselves how they do that and put that in this column (e.g. the priest, the parish AGM, the PCC, etc.). Column (e) reminds us that sometimes the controls are held by those who hold the purse strings. Asking how it is funded is often a good route into the background to a project or activity, too.

Reviewing this kind of list will help the readers unpick what is really happening in the parish (e.g. who has responsibility and who holds authority). We have already stressed how important it is in a community to spread the load. Partly, this is because we want to avoid 'burn-out' in those who contribute so much to the parish. Partly it is because it is more efficient and practical. Being too heavily reliant on a single person or small group will inevitably result in gaps when the pressure is on, when someone is unwell, is forced to leave, or dies.

From your long list you will be able to see where the keys to the parish lie. Do all of the lines of responsibility run to one person or a small group of people? If so, how heavily do all of these activities really rely on that person or small group? One of the problems experienced in parishes where a strong group, leader or priest is the central hub for everything is that communications will tend to be one way. The centre ends up controlling all outward communications. This may be something that the group or individual feels is acceptable, but it is an inadvisable approach to adopt. Chapter 7 looks at communications in more detail.

So, when you considered what kind of parish you might be part of in Chapter 1, you will have made some basic assumptions. Have these been supported by the evidence you now have in front of you? If not, how does it differ? Even if the evidence fits the assumed pattern for your parish, now that you have had the chance to review how the parish works, can you see problems? Can you begin to understand where some of the difficulties experienced in your parish might lie? Problems arise when all paths lead to one person or small group (for example, virtually all of the people in columns (c), (d) and (e) are the same). This both restricts the opportunities to do more in the parish (they can only do so much!) and restricts involvement (they are so busy trying to keep everything together that they cannot recruit and train new people as well) except at the very basic levels. This may not be a problem, of course, and may be how the parish wants to operate. However, unless the parish is a very small one, you are likely to encounter difficulties with this approach.

Another problem that this review can highlight is that responsibility is held by localized or isolated groups and there is no opportunity to co-ordinate parish efforts and plan them effectively.

Conclusions

Exploring how your parish works, even at this simple level, can reveal interesting issues. Parishes are places where personal growth and development can be nurtured and realized. One of the tasks for those who wish to build or regenerate their parish might be to look at how the parish structures help or hinder parishioners in their personal and shared journey towards a knowledge of the risen Christ and a life that follows his teachings.

Perhaps a general aim for every parish should be that they adopt a balanced approach where the maximum numbers of people can be involved and contribute and where the vision and nature of the parish are both understood and shared by the greatest majority of those in the parish.

3

What is Your Parish Really Like?

We do not use deception, nor do we distort the word of God. On the contrary, by setting forth the truth plainly we commend ourselves to every man's conscience in the sight of God.

2 Corinthians 4.2–3

Introduction

The first two chapters have been looking at parishes in general and encouraging the reader to take a careful but personal view of the parish. Now it is time to use more structured ways of looking at and listening to your parish.

Learning about a parish should be something that is shared by as many people as possible within the community. This can be done by sharing the efforts involved in surveying the parish and by sharing the results with as many people as possible. By making it a parish-centred set of activities, much can be done to bring the community closer together.

Surveying the parish can be as broad as it is detailed. Information can be gathered from as many sources as there are parishioners, and then some! Even past parishioners and local schools can take part in the work if that is what the parish wants. You can also find out about the people of the parish and explore the parish's origins and history, its boundaries and so on. Changes in parish life lie in the stories and memories of older parishioners, and their experiences can be contrasted with those of today.

So, surveying the parish can be more intimate and detailed than first expected. We can use it to set the context for understanding the needs and aspirations of parishioners today and see how they can be served in the future. Whatever the parish decides to do, the results can be displayed in the church, hall, local school and even in the local library. There can be articles in the local paper and other local media, and the parish may even produce accompanying booklets which can serve to promote the parish and evangelize.

So, where do you start?

Some basic sources of information

What we know about our parish will be determined by our position and experience within the parish. So, a mother of three young children may have a very different experience and perception of the parish from a retired businessman – even if they have both been members of the parish for the same length of time. The priest's experience and understanding of the parish may be very different from that of a member of the Parish Council.

It seems wise to seek out at least some reliable information before we begin any discussion on the parish. Most parishes will have some useful records to start with and we can build up a useful picture of the parish with their help. There are a number of other sources that may also be available to us, as described below. Once we have examined these, the reader might discover that there are other sources for their parish that have not been listed here.

We have divided the sources into three general types. *Formal parish sources* are those with some kind of structure and background information supporting them. The word 'formal' relates to the way in which the information was gathered (the information is representative of the group it was collected from and is a reasonably reliable and accurate set of records). *Informal parish sources* are those where measurement is not really part of the process and the information is informative but may not represent all groups or views. They provide useful insights and important expressions of feeling, etc. *Non-parish sources* tend to help place all of the other information into the wider context of the community within which the parish exists.

Formal parish sources

These include:

- *Parish records*. Most parishes have a number of different types of record ranging from the information on births, marriages and deaths, through information on baptisms, First Communions, Confirmations, to rotas, memberships of various groups, mailing lists for specific things, and so on.
- *Parish census*. Hopefully carried out on a reasonably regular basis, the census aims to be an accurate record of all parish members along with some personal and other details. The value of this can vary according to the information's age and the quality of the actual census questionnaire, its administration and how the information is stored.
- *Parish accounts*. There may be some useful information here related to who gives what, when and how, which may be effectively summarized in order to add to your understanding of the parish.
- *Previous parish surveys*. Your parish may have carried out a survey to collect information on a particular topic or gather views on parish aspirations, likes/dislikes, and so on. Any such surveys could hold valuable information.
- *Other sources*. Once reviewed, the parish may also hold other records or sources of information of use in your review of what the parish is really like.

Informal parish sources

These may include:

- *Records of parish meetings*. These may link with the more formal sources as they may accurately record the numbers of people involved in various activities. In the context of informal sources, these records may provide useful insights into what people within particular groups think and feel.
- *Reports from groups*. These can be related to the first source in this section, providing information at a more limited and specific level.

- *Newsletters/magazines/publications.* Parishes should have a number of such publications and these can provide useful, historical information.
- *Views from different officers/individuals in positions of responsibility.* Although informal and not measurable in terms of accuracy or how representative the views expressed are, this is an invaluable area of sources giving insight and a useful sense of feeling.
- *Notes, letters, e-mails, phone calls.* Although not representative, these can add some depth to your understanding behind issues facing the parish.
- *Active listening.* Members of the Parish Council or other groups can agree to spend time actively listening to the views and feelings of the parish while enhancing this through careful probing and questioning.
- *Specific meetings/forums.* Informal information can be gathered for specific purposes through the calling together of specific meetings or through joining formal meetings being held by particular groups. This can be very useful for those wishing to consult the parish as well as by those who wish to gain insights, feedback and feelings from particular groups.

Non-parish sources

There can be many of these but they will vary from parish to parish:

- *The National Census.* This provides useful information on your local area. It may not relate exactly to your parish but it will give you details on the area in general which can be compared to information you have already gathered (for example, you might compare the local area's age and gender information with those of your parish). There is a website which allows the public access to a range of information on their local area on-line (see their website at http://www.statistics.gov.uk/census/default.asp).
- *Local authority sources.* Local authorities often have planning and other information which can be related directly to your parish area. In addition to providing more local information it may help you

understand how things have changed locally in the past few years and how things are changing in the near future.

- *Agencies*. There may be other sources of local information from agencies operating in your parish area. Details such as levels of homelessness, child poverty, age issues, drug and crime figures and so on may also be reasonably accessible and enlightening.
- *Schools*. Alongside the agencies, schools can provide useful background information and, if there are church schools serving the parish's area, additional information may be even more useful.
- *Diocese*. Always worth seeking information from further up the chain of command. Dioceses, along with some (national) church bodies may be a useful source, too.
- *Commercial data sources*. Many different companies collect and collate data at local as well as national levels. It is always worth exploring the possibilities in this area. For example, one parish approached a commercial database company located in their area and asked them if they could provide some analyses of the parish and its population. The company used the request as a training exercise and, in addition to providing useful reports, the company developed a strong relationship with the parish.

Location, location, location

How can a parish get to know more about its neighbours?

First, you need to know the area covered by the parish. The parish should have a boundary map but if your parish has only one or has a very old version, now is the time to make a new one. Simply obtain an Ordnance Survey map and mark out the parish boundaries on it (from the original map). You may find that one of the local estate agents or the local authority planning office will be able to provide you with a suitably mounted large-scale map for this purpose. Some estate agents have even been known to donate large aerial photographs of their area mounted on board.

Once you have a fresh map to work with, be careful how you mark it up. The best idea is to do the initial marking with a soft lead pencil so that mistakes can be erased easily. Then you can either mark up the map with a marker pen, carefully rubbing out the pencil marks as you go. Better, still, buy a large sheet of clear acetate or similar plastic film and use it as an overlay for the map. Fix it at the top with pins or sticky tape and trace the boundary with a suitable marker pen before lifting the overlay and erasing the pencil marks.

From your local planning office or from the Office for National Statistics (check out their website at http://www.statistics.gov.uk/census/default.asp) you can obtain information on where the census areas are and what sort of information you can obtain about your local area. By matching up census information to the area of your parish you will be able to build up a good picture of what your local population is like. You can then compare the general population of your area with the characteristics of parish members (from your census or once you have carried out some basic survey work).

The map can be used to explore the context of your church within the local population. Here are some of the questions you could be asking and trying to answer by marking things on the map (or on transparent overlays).

Where are:

- The *other churches*?
- Other *places of worship*?
- *Community facilities* such as community halls, health centres, fitness centres, swimming pools, libraries, parks, hospitals, police and fire stations, etc.?
- *Other social provision* such as old people's homes and sheltered accommodation, special clinics, social service offices, job centres, advice centres such as the Citizens' Advice Bureau, etc.?
- *Education establishments* such as local primary, secondary and other schools, nurseries and child-care centres, colleges, universities, etc.?
- *Public transport provision* such as railway and bus stations, bus/tram routes, and so on?
- *Shopping and entertainment centres* such as the main shopping streets, local shops, out-of-town retail provision, hotels, restaurants, petrol stations, supermarkets, etc.?

- *Commercial centres* such as office blocks, retail/warehouse parks, factories, business parks, etc.?
- *The different types of housing* such as the housing estates, the big detached houses, terraced properties, etc.?

Of course, the list above is just a prompt. You need to consider what is important to you as a community. Rural parishes may include farms, country houses, inns, etc., while very industrial/urban parishes may have little public open space.

Again, the strengths of carrying out this exercise are that it allows members of the parish time and opportunity to explore their area in ways they may not have even considered before. They will find that in so doing they will develop a better understanding of what makes their area special, and this will help them build an even stronger affinity for it.

The resulting map will show whether the church and its facilities are at the geographic centre of the community or at its periphery. You can ask how the location of different parts of the community's facilities and services affects how the parish is viewed by the rest of the community. Sharing the findings with the rest of the parish will lead to better understanding and positive discussions.

Simple things such as the change in a bus route or the location of a shopping centre can affect the day-to-day life of a church.

The information from the census can be displayed alongside the map along with other information (photographs, details of community services, etc.). Simple representations of the information are best. One of your team should be able to produce coloured bar or pie charts showing the characteristics of the local population.

Involving schools in aspects of this exercise can produce exciting and interesting results. Children can produce wonderful maps, models and galleries of pictures of the parish area.

Sharing who we are

Surveying a population can take a number of different forms. It does not always require you to design and fill out questionnaires. Here is a simple example of what we mean.

In one parish they asked the question, 'Where do our parishioners come from?' To answer this they took a copy of their large parish map and put it in a prominent position at the back of the church. They produced flags made from pins with strips of paper attached and invited people to write their surnames and post code on the flags and pin them on the map. Over a period of a month they were able to encourage the vast majority of the parish to leave their flags on the map. There was always someone on hand to help people find their street and put their pin in roughly the right spot.

In the end they were able to show everyone how parishioners were spread across the area. One of the things they were able to do was to identify whole neighbourhoods where there was no link to the church. The parish response was to design a leaflet with a general invitation to visit the church, attend a service and so on. Dates, times and key details were included and an attractive photograph of the church was used to illustrate the leaflet. Parishioners distributed the leaflet door to door in all the areas they had identified from the map.

Several new parishioners joined as a result of that initial activity and the parish see this outreach activity as a regular part of parish life now. One simple question helped to build community, focus people's efforts and successfully evangelize! This was achieved by keeping things simple, involving as many people as possible and communicating the results well.

Recording and attempting to understand the information gathered is just as important as collecting the information properly. In this example, people made a permanent record of the findings from the map and compared the information with other data on the parish area. As well as identifying new housing, areas with people of other faiths and so on, the parish looked at how public transport and road patterns affected access to the church.

Listening more

We have looked at gathering local history, as recounted by older members of the parish, and seen how this can benefit the parish. Using a variety of approaches (including 'story telling') you can explore how different groups of people currently experience being members of the parish. This can be a very valuable precursor to developing a parish questionnaire. In professional research terms you would be gathering 'qualitative' research (information which provides insights, depth and perspective to the subject being studied but which does not provide measurable results) before designing and collecting 'quantitative' research information (information that is measured and representative of the population being studied).

The ways of gathering and using this information can be as varied as the population of your parish. The issues connected to this approach are as follows:

- You cannot assume that any expressed views, feelings and opinions are representative of the majority of the parish, but it will highlight some of the strongly felt views and concerns in the parish.
- The information will help guide you in how to ask questions as well as what questions to ask.
- It should provide the range of views you might want to measure.
- It will add emotional and spiritual content to the other information you gather.
- It can be reviewed again after the survey in order to illustrate what people mean and the context of people's responses.
- You can use it to collect private views or sensitive views which people might find hard to express.

How can this be done?

Here is a range of simple ways of collecting this sort of information.

Individual stories, gathered as recordings, in a scrapbook or similar medium, as personal statements dropped into a sealed box or sent by post, as stories shared in small groups, and so on. Use clear but reasonably open topics and invite people to give (named or anonymous) accounts in response. In some cases, photographs and old copies of newsletters etc. can be used as stimuli.

For more specific questions, invite people to be *interviewed* for a period of five to ten minutes each and record their responses on a tape recorder. The interviewers would have a short list of topics to use as prompts to ensure that every person who is interviewed covers the same territory. Each person doing the interviewing would record very basic information before the interview (age, gender, family situation, length of time in parish, level of involvement in parish life) and make very basic notes to accompany the interview itself. Make sure the notes can be easily identified with the interview for further reference later.

We can use parish equipment such as a *video camera* to allow parishioners to record their views in a video 'booth' or room. The room could contain instructions and prompts (where to sit and face, how to turn the camera on and off, the kinds of areas they should cover, time limits, etc.). They could even fill in a short form before starting the camera (with general information similar to above).

We can use a *large book of lined paper* as a tool for people to express their likes, dislikes, fears, hopes and so on in writing. They could be asked to say who they were, either by giving their name, or, most likely, by giving very brief details (e.g. mother of three, over 45, recent convert). People could be encouraged to say anything they want to say and, if they think of something else, go back and write more.

A *simple open-ended questionnaire* can be used with simple, clear and open questions followed by lots of empty space for parishioners to record their thoughts, experiences and feelings. The open questions should be invitations to comment without trying to guide or influence the respondents in any way.

For *younger people* whose writing skills are still forming we can still provide simple forms which invite them to express their feelings and experiences in drawings as well as words. This can work very effectively, immediately showing how the younger parishioners feel and think about their parish.

Gathered wisdom can be obtained through *group discussion or focus groups* where you invite particular groups of people together to discuss how they experience life in the parish and what they feel about it. Remember that the larger the group, the harder it is to manage. Sometimes it is best to gather together people who are similar and at other times it is better to have a range of different types of people in a group. In most cases we would expect you to bring together people of a similar age or background and gender. You will need to provide some guidance or a list of topics for the discussion and your task as the facilitator will be to make sure everyone gets a chance to speak.

Larger gatherings can be used for this purpose, too. In public meetings, for example, you can split the gathering into small groups and get them to discuss specific topics or problems. You then collect findings when the meeting comes together again.

We have been exploring in this section one area of information gathering and sharing within the parish. The other approach, that of carrying out formal surveys, is our next topic.

Formal or 'quantitative' information gathering

The most direct way of learning more about your parish is to carry out a survey. Formal surveys can cover parish life and activities, parishioners' feelings and interests, and explore expectations and aspirations within the parish. We say this is a 'formal' approach because it is a highly structured process that is approved by the parish and is also planned, organized and carried out with great care and thought.

The word 'quantitative' is the technical term for the kind of survey referred to here. It refers to the form of research which is designed to produce representative and measurable information. It should produce information that is representative of your parish as a whole and which tells you the size and nature of different groups, activities and views within the parish.

Why have a survey?

Surveys will help you:

1. find out more about who the parishioners are and what they are like;
2. find out who does what within the parish;
3. ask people why
   - they are parishioners;
   - they are/are not involved;
   - they like/dislike the parish;
   - they are satisfied/unhappy with the parish;
   - they are/are not fulfilled;
   - want change/want this to stay the same and so on;
4. ask people what they want, like, need, seek, prefer, hate, love, etc.;
5. look at where people want to move to, aspire to, etc.;
6. find out what people are willing to do, going to do, never going to do, and why.

Some of the survey work will be closer to a census (i.e. where you ask *everybody* rather than a sample), or will be the process of recording numbers – who, how many and so on – and will be done on a routine basis (every year or set number of years). Some will be looking at sub-groups within the parish and others will be looking for comments, feelings, ideas or answers to particular problems.

In all parish survey work the focus should be on quality, so that the survey does justice to the people it serves, and is centred in care and love. It should have clear objectives and should always be designed to listen to what people have to say. It should never have questions which encourage or push people into giving particular responses.

What does a survey involve?

There are four basic stages to any survey: the design stage, the distribution stage, the analysis stage and the reporting stage. The most important guideline is to avoid complexity and over-simplification.

We can see how these stages apply to the different types of surveys and get a feel for how they might help your parish.

1. Design stage

   Most researchers will tell you that this is the most important stage of all. Agree the objectives, make sure they can be achieved, and keep to them throughout the design stage. Keep the questionnaire simple, make it clear, make sure you cover all the possible responses to a question and keep it as short as possible. Make certain you can get the questionnaire to all concerned and collect responses, too. Test the questionnaire first on different types of people, time how long they take to complete it and listen to what they have to say. Don't argue with them – solve the problems they point out. Remember that you are going to have to make sense of the responses that come back. Work out how you are going to handle the data before you finalize the questionnaire.

2. Distribution stage

   This combines distribution and collection because one usually determines the other. The questionnaires may be presented at Sunday services and introduced by the priest or leader with the intention of being completed and collected at that service. They may be handed out at meetings or in the hall, they might be posted or hand-delivered to people's homes or put up on the parish website. They may even be kept on a clipboard and the questions asked by interviewers in any of the above contexts.

   How they are distributed and gathered will affect the response rate (the numbers who complete and return it compared with the number you distributed it to) as will the length, complexity and design of the questionnaire and the subject matter it contains.

   Make sure you know how long the questionnaire will take to complete. Always leave plenty of time for gathering in completed questionnaires. Otherwise, people will not finish completing them, will take them away to 'fill them in later' and so on.

3. Analysis stage

You thought about this at the design stage so you should be ready for the completed questionnaires. The fewer 'open-ended' questions, the easier it will be to count responses and be clear about the results.

It may be that a small team or an individual is appointed to do the analysis but it is certainly wise to review the results before reporting back to the parish as a whole. This gives you time to gain the best understanding, test the results against different views and make absolutely certain that what you are going to present is the best, most accurate and honest report of the data provided by the survey.

4. Reporting stage

This will be determined by the survey. Major investigations of parish life, etc. will probably be best presented formally to the whole parish at a meeting or series of meetings as well as in report form. Other approaches may include producing displays, summaries and even workshops to examine the survey results. Aim for the maximum dissemination and optimum understanding of the results.

Changes in policy, direction, goals, focus and so on may be the logical outcome of survey reports. The groups and individuals involved in the survey may also be involved in the changes resulting from it. So, part of the reporting stage may include outcomes and action points which need to be addressed in future.

5. Action/review stages

We need to be aware that the survey was not an empty exercise: it was designed to tell us useful things. We need to act upon the knowledge we have gathered and we should set times for those actions to be completed and plan for some kind of review to take place at a sensible date after that time.

So, if the survey told the parish that there was a strong need for a Bible-reading class to be set up, the parish probably needs to agree on a small team who can plan and set up this new class. They should be commissioned to prepare the class and set it going by a set time, and the parish should then agree to review how the class is working and if it is fulfilling the needs it was designed to meet.

A *simple example of a survey in a parish*

A good way to understand how to conduct a survey is to look at how another parish has used a survey. In this example, a parish of just over 500 people had decided to plan a mission. During a good, lively meeting it was agreed that a small group would put together a survey which would build a good picture of parish life now, before the mission planning started in earnest. They agreed to report back to a similar meeting in two months' time. This seemed like a very short time, but they had already decided to adopt questions from a survey that had been used in a neighbouring parish. The survey was called 'The Church Life Profile'. It was the largest survey ever undertaken of churchgoers in England and Wales and took place to coincide with the 2001 Census. Although the Catholic Church in England did not take part in this survey a similar survey was carried out by CMS (Catholic Missionary Society) – now CASE (Catholic Agency to Support Evangelisation) – at around the same time. Details of this can be found in the web addresses under CASE at the back of the book.

The team agreed that they needed to gather information about all those who completed the survey questionnaire so that they could tell what kinds of people felt and thought particular things. They were clear that they needed to find out more about people's experience when worshipping in church, but they also wanted to know about their worship and prayer life in general. They wanted to see what their views were on key issues of faith and they wanted to know more about how they came to God and what their expectations and aspirations were. The survey would provide basic information to help them all understand the parish better while helping to point the way forward.

Although this all seemed a bit ambitious, they sat down to put the whole thing into some sort of shape. The basic questions were not easy to agree, but in the end they came up with questions on the following (see NCLS website for further details):

- Gender.
- Age.
- Marital status.
- Education.
- Birth place.

Next, the team decided to find out patterns of attendance, so they asked:

- 'Which service do you normally attend?'
- 'How long have you been a member of the parish?'
- 'How many of your close friends attend church regularly?'
- 'Does your spouse/partner attend this church?'

With these questions, the team felt they would be able to tell a lot about the parish that would be useful. By comparing answers across age, gender and the other basics they would be able to tell the parish a mixture of what they already felt they knew (that the families with young children attended church mainly on Sunday mornings for example) while telling them new things such as how frequently different groups of people attended church, and perhaps give some insight into the link between factors such as friendships and attendance.

The next questions were on spirituality within the community:

- 'How often do you experience the following during church services here?' This covered different spiritual experiences.
- 'Which of the following aspects of our church do you personally most value?'
- 'While you may value many different styles of music, which of the following do you find is most helpful to you when taking part in the worship in this church?'
- 'Preaching in our church is usually very helpful to me in my everyday life.' This covered a range from 'Strongly agree' to 'Disagree'.
- 'My spiritual needs are being met in this church.' This measured agreement to this statement, too.
- 'Do you have a strong sense of belonging to this church/parish?'

Personal aspects of faith were also of interest to the team so they used the following to help them find out more from parishioners:

- 'Which statement comes closest to your view of the Bible?'
- 'How important is God in your life?'
- 'Over the last year, do you believe you have grown in your Christian faith?'
- 'How often do you spend time in private devotional activities such as prayer, meditation, reading the Bible alone, etc.?'
- 'Are you regularly involved in any group activities in this parish?'

The team now had 20 questions. They then decided to add a couple of open questions, partly to give people the opportunity to say something in their own words and partly to explore the future as seen by the parish as a whole:

- 'The parish is about to begin planning a mission to enrich spiritual life within the parish and spread the Good News to everyone who lives within the parish boundaries. What sort of activities and events do you hope to see being developed for the mission? What would you like to see as the outcomes of the mission?'
- 'Please outline the top three things you would like to see changed, improved or introduced to the parish by this time next year.'

With some help on the layout and design, they were able to fit the questionnaire onto four pages of A4 which they printed on A3 and folded to A4. They used the vicar and members of the PCC as critical readers and managed to agree a final draft that could go to a local printer. The final document looked professional and was easy to read.

The team already had agreement to conduct the survey over two weeks and spent an evening talking through the process with a small team of volunteers before the first crucial Sunday.

At the beginning of every service for the next two weeks a brief statement was read out telling everyone that the survey was taking place. Questionnaires and pens were distributed by volunteers at the end of each service to all those who had not yet filled one in, and completed forms were folded and put into large sealed cardboard boxes with wide slits on their lids (very much like ballot boxes). People were not allowed to take the questionnaires away to complete at home. If they could not spend the five to ten minutes or did not want to take part they were not hassled in any way. The aim was to capture as many voices as possible and so everyone was given ample opportunity to take part when they felt they could. Everyone was thanked for their help.

The questionnaires were completed in large numbers in the first week and, although the numbers reduced in the second week, the team was still surprised to see just how many more came in. Time constraints meant they kept to a fixed period of two weeks and they did not deviate from that. They counted 396 responses from an estimated 500-strong parish – roughly 79 per cent response rate. Everyone was extremely pleased with the results so far.

Analysis was not as easy as the team had hoped. Putting all the responses onto a spreadsheet allowed them to count responses for every part of every question, which was an excellent start. However, their database expertise was too limited for them to take computer analysis any further. They finally decided on a very simple but time-consuming approach for the more detailed analyses. After agreeing the different tables they wanted in the report, they gathered together in the church hall on a Saturday morning and proceeded to separate and count responses manually, filling in the figures table by table. Although it took some time to do, this approach left the team with a feeling that they knew the patterns of response very intimately.

For the open-ended questions at the end of the form they typed every answer up alongside the other data on the spreadsheet. They then collected and counted all similar answers under summary headings. From this, they came up with lots of quotes plus some strong indications for particular preferred activities and very specific hopes for the future.

The final report looked very professional. They also produced a PowerPoint presentation and a small leaflet summarizing the findings. It gave the team the opportunity to give the parish confidence to start planning the mission. It also boosted the vicar's confidence and enthusiasm, which was an outcome worth having on its own.

The survey results then became part of the narrative of the parish as a whole and was used to help develop a better vision and plan for the future. It seemed to open the door to greater involvement by the parish in a number of other areas of parish life and another survey was pencilled in for some time after the mission.

Conclusions

Gathering information and listening to the people in the parish is, at its most basic level, what we all do. Having a more structured and formal approach allows us to build a more reliable and useful framework of understanding about our parish. This can form the foundation for a parish that is more involving, creative and responsive to its parishioners' needs.

It would seem that the process of doing the research can be as useful and as powerful as reporting the findings. This should not be a surprise, as what we are doing is finding ways of listening to each other more intently. If we can hear what our fellow parishioners are saying, we can begin to work together better. If we work together better, we stand a greater chance of building that kingdom we all want to see.

4

Auditing: Another Approach to Discovering Your Parish

Suppose one of you wants to build a tower. Will he not first sit down and estimate the cost to see if he has enough money to complete it?

Luke 14.28

Introduction

So far, we have looked at what parishes might be like and used a number of tools to help us look more closely at our own parish. We have used observation and listening, we have mapped and discussed, recorded and researched, surveyed and analysed, and gradually a picture has emerged of what our own parish is like and who the players are within it.

The next task is to take stock of all that makes up your parish. From the smallest to the biggest detail, from the simplest task to the most complex, we can do what some people call 'counting and accounting' so that we know exactly what we have to deal with when we talk about how to manage our parish. This process is also sometimes called auditing, but in the parish context we would like to 'count and account' for the less tangible things as well as the physical items in the parish. And just as we did with the other forms of enquiry in the previous chapters, we would like to see the process adding to people's experience of being part of the parish. It should be a positive, affirming experience where we are given the opportunity to have our voices heard and feel affirmed and applauded for our contributions to the parish as a whole.

So, this kind of auditing will be more about taking stock rather than about stocktaking.

What is an audit?

In its broadest sense, an audit is the reviewing of all that you have, all that you do, all that you can claim to have achieved and all that you affect and that influences you. It can include physical things such as buildings, equipment and so on, human resources, the number of active and non-active parishioners, the talents available to the parish, the different groups within the parish, financial things such as money in the bank, money coming in, money being spent and needed, and less easily measured but important things such as levels of satisfaction, spiritual activities, levels of contact with the broader community, and so on.

In its simplest form, audits are just long checklists that help you review what is there but the best form of auditing helps you think about what you are recording and measuring, how you are doing it, and why. It is a learning process which forces you to engage with the detail.

Why audit?

If your intention is to make sense of your parish and try to manage it in a manner that is most effective and satisfactory, an audit will really help. Two of the most common and beneficial outcomes of the audit are as follows:

- A realization that the parish is achieving a tremendous amount – more than anyone had previously appreciated.
- The discovery of areas not so well covered or addressed as expected and the opportunity to make immediate improvements or changes to solve problems.

If these were the only outcomes then the audit would be worth doing, but they are by-products. If you want to manage your parish properly, you are going to have to do your audit first.

Who should perform the parish audit?

If we do this well, the parish audit will involve many different groups and individuals. If we can, we should take advantage of the process to involve as much of the population of the parish as possible.

The first issue addressed by the audit is what to include. We cannot restrict ourselves to purely physical things or to fiscal or economic assets, so the discussion about what should be included is likely to involve the whole parish. The audit we seek to initiate is a review of the spirit as well as the body, the soul as well as the mind, of the life as well as the fabric of the parish. At its best, while providing the basis upon which to build and develop the way you run your parish, it will also generate a great deal of self-examination.

So, we need a process which involves as much of the parish as possible, and a framework to help open up discussion and ensure that nothing important is left out. The following sections will help you with the process and the list.

The steps towards an audit

The people

While the aim might be to involve everyone, there will need to be a group or team who are assigned the task of facilitating the process as a whole and (possibly another group) who will bring the information together and report on it. Direction in forming these groups may come from the Parish Council or some similar body, or it may come from the priest. How they are formed is of less importance than who is in them and what their remit is as a group.

Suggested approaches to finding members of these groups include:

- announcing for volunteers during Masses;
- putting notices in the parish newsletter;
- placing posters and leaflets in the church and hall;
- approaching individuals based on the parish census forms (or similar);

45

- appointing two key members of the Parish Council to gather a team together;
- inviting volunteers from existing parish groups (St Vincent de Paul Society, RCIA, Mothers' Union, Youth Club, etc.);
- instituting a formal parish meeting where volunteers are signed up.

The make-up of these teams should be carefully considered in order to ensure that you have members who can:

- relate to all the disparate groups in the parish (more than one member required for this);
- talk with, encourage and listen well;
- gather information reliably;
- record information in a database or similar (at least one person on the team should be able to do this);
- be willing and able to give time to this project;
- be willing and able to work in a team.

Ideally the teams together should reflect the parish as a whole. For the parish to feel that an unbiased and thorough audit has taken place, the teams will need credibility with, for example, the younger as well as the older parishioners.

The process

Before engaging the parish as a whole in the audit, the team or teams need to develop their idea of what they are exploring and measuring. This will require more than one meeting involving reflection, prayer, debate and idea-storming.

- *Reflection*, on what their parish is, what it is for, what it contains, what it does and so on. The next section will help with this.
- *Prayer*, to give focus to the teams and give them the help and guidance they will need to be both open to the rest of the parish and determined enough to do the best job possible.
- *Debate*, in order to come to a shared vision of what they are doing

and why they are doing it, how they will do it and who will be playing which roles.
* *Idea-storming*, to open up and keep open the scope of their audit.

Once they feel comfortable with what they are trying to achieve, the teams will be ready to take the audit to the parish as a whole.

Consultation

Although open parish meetings are a useful and desirable aspect of consultation, it is not the only approach that should be adopted in order to involve the broadest range of parishioners. Remember, one meeting at one time and place will not be suitable for all of the parish.

Another drawback to public meetings as the prime route to involvement is the nature of these meetings. Even the best ones can still exclude the shy, nervous or frail, and may over-emphasize the views of the most vocal. It may stifle debate and limit the scope of what is to be considered.

A process which might help broaden and deepen involvement would include the following:

* *Group consultation*. Members of the audit team could visit each parish group during one of their meetings and engage the group in discussion through explaining what the audit team are trying to do, how the group can contribute, guide or facilitate their discussions, and collect information from the group. The group could then continue discussion and agree a group view which could be presented to the audit team.
* *Individual consultation*. A brief leaflet describing the audit and a questionnaire inviting views, suggestions and so on could be distributed at Masses and collected before the congregation leave (similar to many churches' approach to the parish census).
* *Prayer and consideration*. During this activity the parish as a whole should be invited to pray for the success of the audit, should be encouraged to examine the roles they play within the parish, and what they get from as well as what they give to the parish.

- *Public parish meetings*. More than one meeting, held at suitable times in order to enable as many people to attend as possible. These would be held after the first two stages in order to share the findings so far, allow the parish to respond and fill in gaps, debate issues of priority and so on.
- *Report back*. The final report, in summary form, to the parish as a whole and in greater detail to those concerned with managing the parish or aspects of it. The report will show how the varied elements of the parish come together, how they contribute to parish life as a whole and where the focus of the parish lies. It will also show where the aspirations of the parish are and where the parish has indicated that its future lies. It should be a subject for further prayer and reflection and used to develop parish-wide consultation and involvement.

This process will take at least a few weeks to complete, possibly a number of months. With almost everybody involved doing this in their spare time and with the problems of finding a suitable time for teams and groups to meet, it is only natural that the process will take longer than an audit in an organization.

If you wish to use the process to build and develop involvement and commitment which can then be utilized later in the management process, then it is important that the audit is done well. To help, the teams involved should draw up a timetable which they can achieve and which ensures that all of the stages are done properly. Figure 4.1 gives an example of such a timetable.

Figure 4.1. Audit team timetable of agreed meetings and events.

Meeting/actions	Notes	Date/time
Commissioning service	Priest/vicar invites the parish to join in commissioning the teams to do the audit.	Sunday, Week 1
Team meeting 1	Outline of objectives, prayer, reflection and team building, initial plans.	Tuesday, Week 1
Team meeting 2	Members share their ideas, lists, etc. and brainstorm further ideas.	Tuesday, Week 2
Team meeting 3	Reflections and prayers on the agreed framework to start the audit.	Tuesday, Week 3
Group consultations	Members of the teams meet, share ideas and facilitate discussions with parish groups.	Weeks 4, 5 & 6
Group feedback	Teams incorporate group feedback into their framework, agree content/structure of forms and survey materials.	Week 7
Parish survey	Agree with priest/Parish Council and print all survey materials and leaflets.	Week 7

Meeting/actions	Notes	Date/time
Parish surveyed	Carry out surveys and other activities.	Weeks 8, 9 & 10
Survey analysis	Data collected and analysed, results incorporated in the audit.	Weeks 9 to 11
Parish meetings	Initial report from the audit, split into groups during meeting and group feedback/ reactions recorded.	Weeks 12 and 13
Final report	Report produced and agreed by parish teams and groups as well as by PCC and priest. Summary produced.	Weeks 13 to 15

Smaller parishes, less ambitious parishes and incredibly efficient and interconnected parishes could shorten this and simplify the whole thing. The aim here is to give you the ambitious whole and leave you to take what is required by or is possible in your parish at the present time.

Parishes without the benefit of a parish priest may find this process illuminating in all sorts of new ways as the community explores its current position.

Building the framework

Some people run their lives with lists and others shun them with great disdain. Those with a dislike of lists should not be disheartened as this framework is a lot more open, especially in its initial stages. There is work for both list-lovers and list-haters in parish audits.

The first task in building a framework is to agree the parts that make up the whole. Some of these are relatively easy to agree and to audit.

These might include all of the physical elements of the parish – the things, the places or the finances – that are recordable, verifiable and measurable. The team will have to be careful to ensure that all of these aspects of the parish are properly recorded and understood. In some cases this can produce surprising and alarming results. For example, one parish on a similar exercise discovered that the statue in their church's Lady Chapel was extremely valuable and in another parish it was discovered that the relationship with the neighbouring school extended into a very old and complicated form of shared ownership of some of the land and properties (a fact that the previous priest had not shared with the new one and which presented major legal and financial problems).

Less easily measured elements might include recording details of the people in the parish, parish activities, relationships within the parish, within the diocese, with local and national communities, parish needs, the 'inputs and outputs' of the parish, and so on. Some of these will be identifiable and measurable elements of parish life, and others will need to be identified, defined, measured and recorded by the team and via parish groups for the team. This is where the core of parish deliberation and involvement may take place. For example, simple questions such as, 'How much interaction does your parish have with your local community?' can cause considerable debate. In one such exercise it was shown that a parish had never really considered the extent to which they were involved in their local community despite the fact that their hall and other facilities had been regularly used by over a dozen different local groups and that there were several parish representatives on a wide variety of different local community groups and committees.

Figure 4.2 gives some major areas to consider when building your framework. From these topic areas we can begin to produce a set of headings under which we can then list relevant items, people, groups, elements and so on.

Figure 4.2.   Major areas to include in the audit framework.

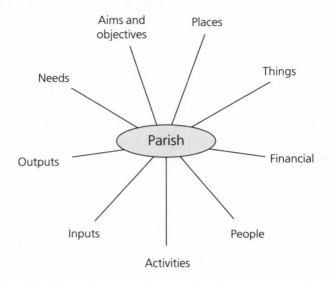

Here are some details developed from Figure 4.2.

Places

- The church.
- The hall.
- Presbytery, Vicarage, Rectory, etc.
- Parish offices.
- Parish shop.
- Parish club.
- Scout hall.
- Other premises.

Things

- Religious items (all valuable items including chalices, candlesticks, etc. kept in the church).
- Special church 'furniture' including altars, tabernacles, etc.

- Other religious items including statues, works of art, etc.
- Furniture – by their location, including pews, hall furniture, etc.
- Technical equipment – including all sound systems, microphones, instruments, etc.
- Other equipment.
- Office furniture and equipment if not above.
- Office goods, supplies and materials, including paper, inkcartridges, etc.
- Priest's home items owned by parish.
- Cars, minibus, bicycles and other similar items.
- Communications equipment.
- Computers, etc.
- Items held off-site by parishioners.
- Other.

Financial

Income and assets including:

- Money in bank.
- Money in other places (bonds, investments, etc.).
- Collection and other regular giving.
- Gift Aid and other similar.
- *Ad hoc* giving.
- Contributions from other religious/educational sources.
- Funds from special/religious occasions.
- Funds from appeals, fundraising activities (e.g. jumble sales, raffles, etc.) and similar.
- Shop and sales/commercial income.
- Rental income.
- Other.

Expenditures, including:

- Rent.
- Mortgages and loans.
- Salaries, stipends, etc.

- Utilities at all locations.
- Maintenance.
- Contributions to church including diocese, etc.
- Charitable contributions.
- Equipment and materials for worship.
- Equipment and materials, other.
- Travel.
- Other.

People

Individuals and groups, numbers and roles, including:

- Parish priest (assistant priests).
- Deacon(s).
- Parish sister.
- Pastoral assistant.
- Youth worker.
- Parish organizer/co-ordinator.
- All other parishioners with a special (religious) role (e.g. Eucharistic ministers, MCs, altar servers, welcomers, musicians/choir, readers, etc.).
- Parish 'staff' paid/unpaid (e.g. parish workers, cleaners, handymen, secretary, etc.).
- Other staff, non-church (e.g. webmaster, accountants, etc.).
- Pastoral Council.
- Members of Catholic Parish Groups (Justice and Peace, RCIA, Baptism/Formation, First Communion, Confirmation, Youth Club, SVP, Mothers' Union, etc.).
- Regular Mass attenders.
- Other Mass attenders.
- Attached schools and those linked with the parish: governors, parents and pupils, and teachers.
- Dean and other Catholic churches of deanery.
- Twinned/linked parishes.
- Parishioners active in ecumenical and other important external

links (e.g. Churches Together, charities, mother and toddler groups, etc.).

- Ministers of local churches.
- Neighbours in the same road.
- Users of parish social centre/club.
- Institutions served by parish (e.g. prisons, rest homes, hospitals, non-attached schools).
- 'Lapsed' parishioners.
- All kinds of valuable census and related information about who is in the parish, their talents and gifts, and so on.

Activities

Following on from the people: what the parish and parishioners do:

- Masses.
- Other regular worship/services.
- Seasonal events/services.
- *Ad hoc* religious.
- Church/hall-based group activities.
- Home/small group activities.
- Services and other provision in local institutions (e.g. schools, hospitals, homes, prisons, etc.).
- Deanery/diocesan/national activities.
- Ecumenical and other linked services and activities.
- Social events and activities.
- Running the shop, hall, etc.
- Clubs, etc.
- Fundraising.
- Activities linked with other institutions (e.g. schools, etc.).
- Social linked actions.
- Non-religious.

Inputs

All the benefits that the parish and its members receive from their activities. For example:

- *Spiritual*. Important, obvious and difficult but entirely essential! Includes personal and community growth and development, nourishing, teaching, evangelization, etc.
- *Community*. 'What has the parish ever done for me?' as an individual, as a member of a group, as a child/parent/partner, as a member of the village/town and so on.
- *Social*. The network of our lives built around the parish (at least in part), the non-religious areas influenced by the parish, etc.
- *Economic*. Development of social, the benefits from having the schools, old people's homes, mother and toddler groups, AA meetings, etc.
- *Personal*. Those who have been 'saved', who have enjoyed different types of support, who have had solace in times of loss, etc.
- *Church-based*. What the rest of the church and the Christian community feed into the parish.
- *Survey and consultation findings*. What did you find out?

Outputs

- All the benefits the parish and its members give to the rest of the church and the community at large.
- Exploring how the benefits to the parish are also benefits to the rest of the community but spending time separating these out and identifying other areas where the parish serves those outside it.
- What the parish gives to the church as a whole and to the rest of the Christian community.
- The charitable and other work done by the parish.

More will be added from any questions asked in the survey and during the consultations.

Needs

What are the members of the parish and the parish as a whole needing or seeking? Examples might include:

- Developments of the benefits already being offered by the parish.
- New developments identified as important by the parish (e.g. a youth worker, a part-time musician, etc.).
- Greater involvement in aspects of spiritual life (by parishioners generally, particular groups not well served at present, by linked groups such as schools, etc.).
- Physical improvements and developments such as a new hall, new offices, better sound system, etc.).
- Survey and consultation results – what did you learn in these exercises?

The parish's aims and objectives

What do the parish and its groups/members aim to achieve in the coming year(s)? For example:

- Established and planned physical improvements (to the church or other buildings, to equipment, etc.).
- Development and expansion of spiritual guidance, growth, training provision or involvement (RCIA, etc.).
- Addition of new groups seen as important for parish growth (J&P group, Fair Trade stall, re-start Mothers' Union, etc.).
- Expansion of parishioner involvement through increased membership of ministries and similar (for example, increase of Eucharistic ministers, readers, etc. by 10 per cent next year).
- Improved support for all those who have roles of responsibility within the parish (including the priests, deacons, etc.).
- Development of training and mentoring programmes for all parishioners and staff active in the parish's work.
- Development of better management of the parish as a whole.
- Aspirations – based on previous parish reports and discussions, the audit consultations and responses from the parish survey.

Lists, lists and more lists

After thinking about, discussing and agreeing the lists of things to measure, all you have to do is start counting. The teams put their lists into forms, they decide how they are going to do the counting, and then they start doing it. In some cases, this will be quite straightforward. You can count exactly how many people attend each of the different services and other shared worship events during a period of a week or a month, but this will not tell you exactly how many worshippers there are in total. For example, some people may attend a particular service every Sunday and other people may only attend that service once every two or three weeks. There will be a steady flow of people each week which might average out to a broadly consistent figure, but it will be less than the total number who attend over a period of a month. To find out the real count you have to ask the right questions. One way is to ask everyone (over a period of weeks) how often they attend each service, as Figure 4.3 illustrates.

Figure 4.3. Sample of a service attendance question.

Q. How often do you attend each of the following:							
	Weekly services only. In an average month I will attend:			Daily services. In an average week I will attend:			
Details of all the services	One service	Two– three	Four or more	One service	Two	Three– four	Five or more

Another is to have a short form at every service for a period of a month which asks a similar question about that service. Have everyone fill in the form only once, and as well as being able to see how often they claim to attend each service, you can count up the forms for each service and the total will be the total number of people who have attended each service over that period. Compare that with your census or other attendance count records. The difference is the amount your parish regularly underestimates its attendance by! Many parishes have found that as much as one-third more people attend than is normally estimated!

Wherever possible, try to have the people responsible for an event or group involved in the counting. They will be able to point out similar issues regarding counting in their area.

When it comes to accounting for feelings, needs, aspirations and so on, the work you will have already done in planning, designing and carrying out surveys will serve as important experience.

Bringing the mass of data together can be done as one great, co-ordinated task or it can be done incrementally as the work is carried out. With one central place to collect and process the information each time a group or team completes their task, they can perform the basic arithmetic and provide both the completed records and the top-line counts for their area.

The completed forms, their design and spare copies can be stored for reference so that the next audit is easier and so that any measures the parish may want to do again can be done more easily and can be done so that the results are comparable with this latest one.

Sharing responsibility: an example of one part of the audit in more detail

In this example a parish asked the simple question, 'How does a community respond to the needs of its members?' The instinctive answer is that everyone should share responsibility for looking after the community's needs. In practical terms, the way the load is spread will always be uneven. But the instinctive answer is a good one.

Examining how good we are at sharing responsibility can be an interesting and challenging task. The methodology is not complex and a rough test can be carried out by any group within the parish. The first step is to agree a basic principle before you make the assessment.

To agree this principle you have to ask the group this simple, two-part question:

> When does a role or task become burdensome to a member of the community, and what should be the maximum number of times for a person to carry out that task or role in any given month?

The first recognizes the potential for 'burn-out' even in the simplest of roles in a parish. The second recognizes that sharing the burden reduces 'burn-out' and increases involvement.

So, if we examine all the services on a typical Sunday we can count up the number of different roles that are performed by members of the parish (excluding the priest, in this instance). How many people are welcomers and how many distribute books? How many are involved in different ways preparing for, taking part in the service and doing things after the service? If some people do more than one thing during a particular service, decide whether those roles are logically combined or whether they are more normally carried out by different individuals. Count up all of the different roles and tasks for that typical Sunday.

Now, assuming that there are, on average, four Sundays in a month and that any fifth Sundays occurring during the year will be shared out across the people whenever appropriate, multiply the number of roles/tasks by four.

Now look at Figure 4.4. This will help you with the calculations. The numbers in the table are for demonstration purposes only. All you do is record the tasks and how many people are required on Sunday. Multiply each by the number of Sundays per month (four on average), decide the maximum number of times a month people should be expected to do this, and calculate the total number of people required per month. Add them all together and compare it with the number you currently have performing those roles/tasks.

Figure 4.4. Sample table auditing Sunday roles and tasks.

(A)	(B)	(C)	(D)	(E)
Roles/tasks during Sunday	Total numbers each Sunday	Monthly total (B) × 4	Maximum number of times per month	People required per month (C) ÷ (D)
Welcomers	15	60	1	60
Children's liturgy leaders	8	32	2	16
Totals				

The next issue to examine is the amount of preparation, training and support required by each task or role. Some will need very little training and support, others will require a lot. Divide the list you have created according to their required levels of preparation, training and support, and check that the division truly reflects the value of each task or role. For example, at one time people might have frowned at the idea of giving welcomers training and considering it as anything like a form of ministry. In today's world many welcome teams are well prepared and trained.

Alongside this assessment, consider how long the lead time is between someone offering themselves for any one of these given tasks or roles and them actually beginning to carry out the role competently. Again, if some take little or no time it may be because the parish does not regard the task highly enough.

Once this analysis has been completed, we need to ask ourselves another question:

How long should any individual keep on with any given task or role?

For a small number, the answer might be 'for life' as they have accepted a lifetime vocation. They would be in the group whose training and preparation would have been among the longest and most demanding. However, there will be a number where the preparation time will be much shorter but still significant. Many people need to build up their confidence as well as knowledge and experience.

Generally, most organizations think that a period between three and five years should be set on the length of time you spend on committees and management boards. A similar period could be appropriate for most roles within a parish community, too. Think carefully and discuss this as fully as possible before you decide. There may well be roles that should not be carried out for more than a year or two, and others may be ones that relate to specific situations. For example, certain roles may require that you are at a particular stage in your life such as being a parent of young children etc.

Obviously, no community would expect everybody to change roles all at the same time. If we use the five-year span as our basis, one-fifth (20 per cent) each year should either drop out and rest or swap roles or tasks with someone else. Alongside this we may see as much as 10 per cent who will stop performing their task or role completely due to changes in circumstances – moving away, illness, death and so on. Thus, we might expect that between 20 and 30 per cent of those involved during Sundays need to be replaced each year.

The training/preparation timings tell us how long our lead-in per person per task is.

In order to ensure that this fall-out and turnover does not unduly affect the spiritual life of the parish, those involved in planning and managing the rotas, schedules, etc. should be thinking about ongoing recruitment of new people and cultivating a system where there are many more people than the base figure for their activity suggests. So, if you and your colleagues have a base number of 15 welcomers during Sunday (60 for the month) you might be thinking about adding upwards of three 'trainees' or 'support members' to each Sunday team to fulfil both your requirements with regard to training and preparation and to cover the teams as and when people drop out or retire.

One of the startling details often revealed by this exercise is how a very small number of people quite often prop up the parish by giving their time and energies to an excessive degree. As you go through the exercise you might find the same small number of names cropping up as the people doing several key roles every week. This time and effort may be given freely and happily by the people concerned, and the parish can be grateful and celebrate their wonderful contributions. However, this is far from the best, most sensible and most caring approach for a parish to adopt. The reliance on a few for so much leads to a number of problems including the following:

- The parish is relying on an unstable system. It will take just a small set of changes to cause the system to collapse.
- There are likely to be no fall-back positions when the inevitable disaster occurs.
- The parish runs the risk of being responsible for the 'burn-out' of some of its most devoted members.
- Reliance on a small number ensures that the parish remains both inflexible and makes change difficult.
- It is both an inefficient use of the talents of those who have taken on the burden and of those who are not used.
- It excludes many who would otherwise be more involved in contributing to the parish.
- It leaves useful and sometimes vital knowledge and experience in the

hands of a limited number of people, with no mechanism for sharing that knowledge and experience with others, all of which risks being lost through illness, sudden changes in circumstances or even death.
• It often narrows both the experience and the expectations of the parish as a whole.

Being a small parish may not be a good enough excuse to allow this situation to take place. The more spread out a load is, the lighter the load becomes for everyone, and the greater the opportunities to do more as a community. The number of people actively involved in a parish is very often related to the dynamic quality of the parish as a whole. Furthermore, the chances of a parish growing relate directly to the level of dynamism within its community. A parish of 50 leaning on the same half-dozen people to do most of the tasks is a very different parish from a parish of 50 with 30 people active within it.

Sharing the load does more than increase the dynamic quality of a parish so that it can do more: it also helps define the parish as a whole through a mixture of shared experience and ownership. This is key to the parish's ability to survive through difficult times. A parish without a priest, for example, will survive and may even continue to flourish if the principle of sharing the load was already established before the interregnum. Similarly, if any other form of disaster befalls the parish, it will be the strength of the parish as a community, its ability to work together and its shared vision that will help it survive.

So, carrying out an audit of people's roles/tasks on a Sunday (or any other day) will produce information which will help the parish face key issues about how it operates. It is a route to realistic and caring management practices. Multiply this across each and everything counted and the parish as a whole will be accounted for and accountable.

Conclusions

Listing some of the basics involved in the audit reveals the complexity and richness of a parish. It tells us why parishes can be so difficult to manage and reveals just how much of what a parish does is dependent on the time and commitment of particular individuals.

As the audit delves deeper into the workings of the parish itself it does more than count the human and spiritual assets that it finds. It points out the needs and provides opportunities to begin to explore solutions. As our simple example reveals, the heart of parish life depends on the goodwill and dedication of a large number of people doing a wide variety of tasks. And while many of these tasks appear simple, even trivial, they can become enormously burdensome if fewer and fewer people undertake to do them.

5

Considering Management

'I want to give the man who was hired last the same as I gave you. Don't I have the right to do what I want with my own money? Or are you envious because I am generous?' So the last will be first, and the first will be last.

Matthew 20.14–16

Introduction

In this book we wish to concentrate on Christ-centred management, on collegiate approaches to working together and on care, support, love and similar concepts. Exploring this approach leads to the possibility that a successful parish serves the needs of its parishioners by bringing them all closer to realizing the kingdom of God on earth. This book attempts to provide some assistance in trying to achieve that. The coming chapters all explore management in this light.

What do we mean by management?

If we reflect on the meaning of management in the context of Christ, his life and his teaching, we will discover that Christ provides us with a particular kind of blueprint for management. Here is a set of the themes that can be applied to management which are based on Christ's teaching and example:

• Service to others.
• Trust.
• Care.
• Sharing with others.

66

- Challenging and questioning in God's name.
- Openness.
- Honesty.
- Loving God and neighbour.
- Accepting personal responsibility.
- Accepting other people's help.
- Being part of God's family/working together.

The life of the parish is a continual pilgrimage. Being a community means that some people will move faster than others and some will not want to move very far, or at all. So management becomes more than just a way of moving from A to B or setting and achieving a range of traditional management goals.

Let us look at how the themes we have identified apply to management. As we progress through this section of the book we will see how these apply in detail but here are some simple examples.

1. *Service to others*. As Jesus tells us, 'the Son of man himself came not to be served but to serve, and to give his life as a ransom to many' (Mark 10.45) and we have the opportunity to follow him in parish life. Serving in the parish can be as simple as giving someone a lift to the service you usually attend on Sunday. This could free someone else to serve the church in another way. Your act becomes a service to the person you give a lift to, to the person you release from that duty, and a service to the church and God as well.

2. *Trust*. Jesus said, 'I tell you the truth, if you have *faith* and do not doubt, not only can you do what was done to the fig tree, but also you can say to this mountain, "Go, throw yourself into the sea," and it will be done' (Matthew 21.21), so faith (and trust) cannot be dismissed easily. In the context of the parish, trust is one of the pillars holding up the community. Trusting in others ensures that the burden is spread more evenly.

3. *Care*. 'I tell you the truth, whatever you did for one of the *least* of these brothers of mine, you did for me' (Matthew 25.40). Care is a key skill in mainstream management. A good manager is mindful of her or his staff and takes good care of them. As Christians, we

know that care is the positive outcome of love. Care is at the centre of our actions as we respond to being aware of the needs and vulnerabilities of those around us. Care causes us to view decisions in the light of the needs of those around us.

4. *Sharing with others.* Consider Mark 8.6–8. As with everything Christ did, the miracle is both obvious and complex. Was the miracle the fact that Christ turned such a small amount of food into enough to feed everyone and still have seven baskets of food left over? Or was it the act of Christ's sharing that caused everyone to share, too? In effect, both are true at the same time. The miracle is one of Christ's generosity and it is the miracle of what happens when we share. Sharing is a key management skill and an opportunity to witness a miracle in our daily lives.

5. *Challenging and questioning in God's name.* 'So I say to you: Ask and it will be given to you; seek and you will find; knock and the door will be opened to you. For everyone who asks receives; he who seeks finds; and to him who knocks, the door will be opened' (Luke 11.9–10). Jesus challenged the people he encountered, he challenged his disciples and he still challenges us today. By following his example we can do three things. We can ask more of ourselves, we can ask difficult questions, and we can ask God for help and guidance. Remember, challenging and questioning has to be linked with faith, responsibility and care.

6. *Openness.* 'He said to them, "Do you bring in a lamp to put it under a bowl or a bed? Instead, don't you put it on its stand? For whatever is hidden is meant to be disclosed, and whatever is concealed is meant to be brought out into the open. If anyone has ears to hear, let him hear"' (Mark 4.21–23). Openness is easier when you are in a safe, comfortable place and where you know you can trust those around you. Creating such a place may mean that you have to take the risk of being open first. Openness helps to generate openness in others and it fosters trust. When you manage through openness you help to remove barriers and build trust, you see people sharing commitment. Openness also can help to resolve conflicts, reduce resistance to change, transform attitudes and generate understanding.

68

7. *Honesty*. 'You used to be like people living in the dark, but now you are people of the light because you belong to the Lord. So act like people of the light and make your light shine. Be good and honest and truthful, as you try to please the Lord' (Ephesians 5.8–10). Like openness, honesty can be a hard thing to do and can be even harder to receive. The test comes from looking into your own heart and mind and asking if you have been honest to yourself and, especially, to God. Try to start by asking yourself how honest you are about your own motives, feelings and actions.

8. *Loving God and neighbour*. ' "Love the Lord your God with all your heart and with all your soul and with all your strength and with all your mind"; and, "Love your neighbour as yourself." "You have answered correctly," Jesus replied. "Do this and you will live" ' (Luke 10.27–28). This act of love is not something we can be selective about: it is the basis upon which we live as part of the community of the parish and the ruling principle behind how we manage or make decisions in the parish. It is also telling us we should take part in making things happen in our parish and not leave others to shoulder all the burden.

9. *Accepting personal responsibility*. 'His master replied, "Well done, good and faithful servant! You have been faithful with a few things; I will put you in charge of many things. Come and share your master's happiness!" ' (Matthew 25.21). One of the difficult parts of managing is dealing with unco-operative and unresponsive people – especially when you are trying to do things on their behalf or for them. Accept personal responsibility and co-operate. You will see your own (and other people's) lives improve as a result.

10. *Accepting other people's help*. 'So they signalled to their partners in the other boat to come and help them, and they came and filled both boats so full that they began to sink' (Luke 5.7). One of the hardest things to accept is that you might need help. Of course, accepting help carries a risk, and so does offering help. Consider carefully what you are doing when you reject someone's offer of help. Consider all of the gains from accepting it. Generosity can be shown in acceptance as well as in offering.

11. *Being part of God's family and working together.* 'Again, I tell you that if two of you on earth agree about anything you ask for, it will be done for you by my Father in heaven. For where two or three come together in my name, there am I with them' (Matthew 18.19–20). The heart of parish life is being part of God's family. If you believe that to be true it should be important for you to act as if it is so. And being in a family means getting on with others, looking out for each other and sharing in the work.

What emerges from this is a caring and collegiate form of management that seeks to share and distribute burdens. The pattern of daily life in many parishes is often one of a concentration of responsibility and work in too few hands. Also, the drive to be more efficient can be so great that we miss the purpose behind our actions. Sharing may not always appear efficient if the task at hand is the only consideration. If caring and sharing are central to the task at hand, then it becomes inefficient to leave the task to a single, overworked individual or small group.

So, what do we mean by management? Our first answer is that management is a process of working together to try to serve God as best we can within our parish using Christ's teaching and example to guide us. The second is that management is a process of continually trying to improve the way we do things as we make that journey towards realizing God's kingdom on earth. It is not just what we do but how we go about doing it and who we do it with.

Who manages?

We have suggested that management is a shared activity and responsibility. This has several implications and needs to be considered within the make-up and current status of the parish you are in, the rules, requirements and structures of your parish and how they relate to the requirements of your diocese and denomination, and the spiritual beliefs, convictions and hierarchical structures you are required to work within. Although these may all be connected in some way, it is useful to tease them out and examine how they affect what we are trying to achieve.

The parish context

The size and level of activity contained within a parish will affect how management is shared. Once you begin to look at how responsibilities are distributed throughout a parish, you begin to realize that a great deal of responsibility is often distributed across a large number of people. This can be spread across time as well as between locations and within various activities.

The personality and perceived responsibilities of individuals within your parish may be important. For example, an individual who finds it impossible to delegate may end up restricting what is possible by insisting that they have to be present at all activities they feel even peripheral responsibility for. This may also be affected by the views of the priest in charge or the Parish Council's perceptions. Adverse happenings in the past may have caused a hardening of these attitudes or restrictions.

The major question that arises is how the parish manages to balance responsibility with authority. What value is there in being given major responsibilities when you have no authority to carry them out effectively? Management needs to find ways of spreading authority as well as responsibility. So, the parish context may be dominated not by who takes and shares responsibilities but by the person or people who hold the authority and give authority. This leads us to the power structures and hierarchies.

Parish structural elements

In each parish there will be duties and responsibilities which are expected to be confined to specific people. We have already outlined some of the responsibilities of churchwardens, priests and officers in Parish Councils. These need to be recognized and accepted as part of the legal and structural aspects of the parish. Such positions also hold authority.

It is an important lesson to learn that authority and responsibility are not finite. The people at the top do not lose their authority or responsibility when they allow others to share in part of it. For example, a priest's responsibility for the church is not diminished or lost when a cleaner is given responsibility to clean the church.

Hierarchy and church rules

Some issues of management within a parish may be determined by policy and church law, which goes beyond the confines of the parish itself. For example, the current approach in the Catholic Church emphasizes that the authority and responsibility for virtually everything within the parish lies with the parish priest. In practice, priests are not super-human and many responsibilities are shared. How the priest decides to share responsibility and authority will help determine the shape and life of the parish. Of course, the reduction in the numbers of clergy may also affect this whole area in ways still to be decided.

So, where does the answer to the question 'Who manages?' lie? In one extreme (found or implied within the Catholic Church) the answer may be that only the priest can manage the parish. In the other extreme we might say that everyone who wishes to be part of the parish community must accept some degree of responsibility for the parish and therefore become part of the management team.

In practical terms, we need to recognize that it is not an 'either/or' situation. The reality is that parishes, like all communities, contain a mixture of different types of approach operating in conjunction with each other. We can recognize authority, accept that particular individuals hold that authority, and still have situations managed by other people. We can also recognize the difference between spiritual authority and management accounts and between being an elected representative of a community and taking responsibility for part of the cleaning rota. The existence of one role does not negate the other. So, part of the answer is in recognizing that the parish is a mosaic of different types of authority and responsibility, and another part is to recognize that we can decide what sort of mix suits our parish and even decide the mix we want for our parish in the future.

The 'Who manages?' question is therefore determined by the mix we decide upon based on our understanding of the kind of parish you have, the influences that are being exerted on it at the moment and where the parish wants to be in the future.

Decision-making and issues of authority and responsibility

A major theme emerging from this book is how these two aspects of management are handled within a community such as a parish. It is time we unpicked some of the parts and found out what they mean and how they operate within your parish.

Decision-making takes place when people manage situations. We decide between different options, choose courses of action to solve problems or bring about agreed objectives, and so on. We can make decisions as individuals or as groups and we can choose to make staged or stepped decisions as part of this. Thus, we can agree the general principles as a group and then all of the people affected by this decision can then make decisions based on those general principles. The two things we require when making these decisions are the authority to make the decisions and the willingness to accept responsibility for carrying them out. Being given the responsibility is not the same thing as being given the authority. For example, it may be agreed by the parish that the church hall can be hired and used by secular or non-parish organizations at any time apart from Sundays. Hire and use of the hall can then be managed on that basis by a small team who look after the hall.

In this example there are three ways in which this process can be managed in a parish. The first is where the team clean, maintain and supervise use of the hall but make no decisions regarding who uses it. They are key holders but not decision-makers.

The next example has the priest or Council deciding a policy regarding the kinds of people/groups who can hire the hall. The team are then expected to apply that policy. However, they have no authority to change the policy or to interpret it beyond set boundaries. So, their authority is limited and controlled by the policy. Any new situations require the authority of the priest or Council to provide a decision. If the team make decisions beyond the policy boundaries they are exceeding their limited authority.

An alternative scenario sees the priest or Council agreeing a policy with the team. Authority is then passed to the team in a commissioning document which confers authority on the team, recognizing that they are being trusted to take on the management of the hall. They are recognized as having the experience and training to have the authority and responsibilities conferred on them as defined in the document. Their activities can be reviewed and monitored, and when special circumstances arise the team can be trusted to make judgements on their own or decide it is too important or too far out of their remit for them to decide alone. In this case they consult the appropriate higher authority within the parish.

Again, it should be understood that giving someone authority does not necessarily take your authority away from you. However, when authority is given along with responsibility it displays trust in that person or group. It also allows the person or group to act in a way which justifies that trust. Finally, it ensures that the decisions they make are part of the overall authority of the parish and are therefore accepted as valid decisions by others. A chain or sequence of authority is established through which other things such as trust and respect can flow.

Finally, this chain or sequence of authority does not have to be completely hierarchical for it to work. However, without some form of sharing or conferring of authority it becomes very hard to distribute responsibility or allow decision-making to take place anywhere other than at the centre (or top).

Back to management

It may feel daunting, and for some it may even feel inappropriate to suggest that everyone in the parish should be involved in managing the parish. Part of the problem may be the idea of management itself. Many will expect management to be done by someone who has been appointed or has accepted the role of 'the manager'. The other part of the problem is to do with issues of authority and responsibility covered earlier.

The first thing to note is that *management is a process*. It is what ensures that things get done. It is also the way in which different people operate and work together. So a group of people brought together to perform a task need to work out how to divide their labour, work together and time their endeavours in order to complete the task. Although this can be achieved with someone taking control and telling others what to do, it is not the only way in which things happen, and it may not even be the most efficient way to go about doing the task.

So *management can be shared just as effectively as it can be imposed*. The guidelines are that the people involved need to be able, willing and comfortable with the approach that is adopted and it should be the most appropriate approach in the circumstances. If the one adopted is inappropriate then the outcome may be unsatisfactory or even result in failure.

Another thing to note is that changes from one system to another may cause difficulties. These problems can arise purely because of the change but they can also occur when the group is not aware of how it was operating in the first place. So, it can be just as difficult for a group who have worked together co-operatively to adjust to a strict hierarchy as it can be for people working in a highly structured management system to adjust to a co-operative one.

This is illustrated when we consider a parish that has been without a priest or vicar for some time. All of the administrative and management responsibilities usually centred in the priest are soon devolved to members of the congregation and the parish continues to live and perhaps even flourish. If a new priest arrives and this person expects to take back all of these responsibilities and perhaps be involved in making decisions in many other areas, too, how does the parish react? Some people will step back with relief and leave the priest to take on anything and everything he or she was doing during the vacancy. Others will resist and feel that their roles, functions and responsibilities are being snatched away from them. Some will feel that the whole nature of the parish has been changed and there may be deep feelings of disruption, dissatisfaction and uneasiness as a result. This may be manifested in unexpected areas and may cause friction and worse before the system settles down again.

The outcome of the change will vary depending on the style and experience of the priest and the priest's approach to management. Some priests will spend a bit of time taking stock before they make any changes or take on anything but the most basic of responsibilities in the parish. 'Focus on God within the parish first and let everything else fall into place' was the way one priest expressed this approach.

Several methods have been shown to be effective when adopting this approach. For example, one new priest arriving after a long vacancy discovered there was a problem with the connections to the computer in the priest's office. This meant that many of the administrative and other functions continued to be done by those members of the parish who had been doing them for some time. The computer took a long time to get fixed, allowing the priest time to learn much more about how the parish worked, who was doing what, where help was really needed, and who could be safely left to handle different tasks and responsibilities. And, as expressed earlier, it gave the priest the best opportunity to focus on the spiritual life of the parish and begin to build on and develop that without shouldering the burden of lots of other tasks. It also ensured that those who had been at the heart of keeping the parish alive continued to do this – leaving the priest in the position of being able to add to what was already in place. The priest discovered that a number of people would have automatically relinquished their responsibilities if there had not been a ready-made excuse in the non-functioning computer.

In summary, the fact that we work together means that we often have to organize ourselves. Thus management does not have to be centred on one individual. Furthermore, when dealing with a complex structure such as a parish, the management can take different forms depending on the area of activity and what it involves.

Sharing responsibility and even authority does not dilute the priest's or parish authority's power. Empowering others to take on responsibility and authority requires you to know yourself as well as others. It is how we recognize and develop our own as well as other people's talents. It is also how we develop and show trust.

Some notes on managing change

We have suggested that change can be a difficult thing to manage. In general terms this is true, and it is even more evident in parish management.

Change in the parish can be brought about through decisions made by the church authorities. These are usually not for debate once they have been decided and implemented. How the parish adopts and deals with them and how the community works at helping its members adapt becomes the management issue. In this situation the key elements in the change process are to:

- *keep people informed*. This should be done so that no major changes are a surprise. It also gives people the opportunity to ask questions and have everything explained fully before implementation takes place.
- *try to work together*. If you cannot change what is going to happen, you can start working together to prepare for the changes and begin to adapt as you accept. Some may find it hard to 'own' the changes, as some management people would say, but they can start the process of getting used to the change.
- *be patient but be honest*. Some people will still be unhappy about a change well after it has been accepted by the majority. Being patient and considerate will always be an important aspect of dealing with them. However, it is also important that people are honest about the change, too. If the change is not going to be reversed it is not advisable to pander to people's discontent by letting them persist in the belief that things might change back.
- *build on the change*. Once you build new structures based on the change, you can use them to celebrate or enhance the change. Look for new approaches which spring from the change. Let it become an established part of parish life or worship.

Where change is something that has to be negotiated or won (for example, when the majority want the change but a vocal or powerful minority resist) a number of strategies can be adopted. Here is a summary of some of the things you might consider:

- *Try to be open and honest.* The use of peer pressure can sometimes be effective but do not try this if you do not have the facts and weight of argument needed to make it a truthful and honest approach.
- *Try to introduce the changes gradually.* Sudden changes are sometimes resisted even by willing participants. Gradual changes allow for greater development of the content and value of the change.
- *Approach the resistance in stages or group by group.* This need not be a divide-and-rule strategy. In many cases resistance to change will present itself as a wall of common dissent but the wall will be made up of bricks of many different types. Deal with individual difficulties and unhappy groups according to their own particular issues. It is a more sensitive approach and can be very effective.
- *Find areas of compromise that lie outside the changes.* Often people resist change because they want something else which is not really related to the change at all. Identify these forms of resistance and answer their particular needs, and the resistance will often disappear.
- *Deal with leaders or disaffected individuals directly.* Sometimes the problem is not about the change but about the people involved. Does the resistance leader see the change as something that will take away part of their kudos or responsibility? Is the change being led by someone they do not like?
- *Build the case.* This should always be done, anyway. As the change is planned it should be possible to add to the original arguments for it. Look for places where they have already done this and use them as examples.
- *Collect evidence and witnesses.* Alongside the previous point comes the opportunity to present additional facts and figures, produce individuals from other parishes and perhaps other senior people from the diocese.
- *Gather all the reasons against and counter them.* Although this should not be the only approach, it is sometimes one of the things that has to be done. However, avoid being derogatory when countering people's

arguments. Try to answer questions with respect and care and never dismiss mistaken views or prejudice. Use them as opportunities to educate and inform.

- *Find things that are similar and already exist.* In a number of cases, it will be possible to point to other actions, approaches or processes that already exist and have been accepted by the parish. This may build confidence in the change.
- *Make space for dissenters.* Sometimes this is what has to be done to accommodate those who cannot be persuaded. As long as this does not affect the rest of the parish in a detrimental way it may be a good option to consider. However, be very careful and reserve this option for when all else fails.

Readers may be able to add to this list but by working through it as a group you will be able to develop your own strategy for dealing with and managing the change.

More on management styles

Before we move on, let us examine one final aspect of management that often creates problems and issues. Everyone who manages tends to develop their own approach based on their experience, preferences and skills. Problems and conflicts can arise when two or more different styles come together. So what do we need to take note of in the area of management styles?

- *Be aware that there are a number of different management styles.* Consider raising the fact that your style is not the same as another person's when this seems to be presenting a problem. A comparison of approaches may make all the difference to how you work together.
- *Be mindful that different approaches may not mean that different objectives are being sought.* Look at what you are both trying to do and keep the objectives in mind as you settle other differences.
- *Remember that life in a parish is not and should not become a competition.* Where someone's style is competitive or aggressive it needs to be tempered by the situation you are all in.

- *Attributes that are exaggerated or extreme may not best suit management in a parish situation.* This applies to those who are very conservative or cautious in their style just as much as it applies to those who are excitable or impulsive.
- *Management within the parish is not an activity carried out for the manager's benefit.* All who wish to contribute to managing the parish are carrying out a service, not adding to their personal status or power.
- *Abrasive or inappropriate behaviour cannot be excused as 'just being someone's management style'.*
- *Management in the parish context is seldom, if ever, going to be purely about achieving a particular goal and should never be about achieving it at all costs.* If there is no room for love in the plan, the plan needs to change. If there is no love in the style, the style needs to change.
- *Accept that you are not perfect, and look at yourselves critically.* What are you good at and what are you not so good at? Try to focus your activities in areas you are good at and avoid trying to do what someone else can do better.
- *Judge what you are doing and how you are doing it against the principles laid out in the beginning of the chapter.* If everyone does this, there should be few problems.

Try to build on your talents, love your neighbours and try to follow Christ's example.

Conclusions

Management in the parish requires us all to accept some responsibility both in terms of our actions and our understanding. The parish is not simply a business or a charitable institution and what we do to help run the parish has a faith and spiritual dimension to it as well as a community aspect. Getting things done may not be enough: doing things properly might be better. So our style as well as our actions in management need to be centred in serving God's purpose.

Reflecting on the 'Why' and the 'How' we do things as individuals and as groups will help us manage in a more Christ-focused way.

Allow trust to be part of the process and ensure that authority is given where it is needed rather than buried like the Talent in the proverb.

Consider what it means to say that management in a parish is about service, not power.

6

Support and Development Systems

'I have compassion for these people; they have already been with me three days and have nothing to eat. If I send them home hungry, they will collapse on the way, because some of them have come a long distance.'

Mark 8.2–3

Introduction

We have already discussed why managing a parish is not a job for one person. It may be the case that your particular church has a single person who has the role of leader of the parish. However, we have seen that having ultimate authority and responsibility does not mean having to do and run everything. Devolving authority and responsibility is not the same as avoiding or relinquishing it. The very detailed nature and size of some tasks in a parish means that it is inevitable that several people will end up sharing responsibility for making things happen.

Some of this work will be done in groups, teams or committees and other areas will become the responsibility of individuals. In order to ensure that the different parts of the parish continue to work properly there needs to be the following:

- We need to provide *pastoral care* for those with responsibilities and duties.
- We need to debate and decide *the length of time* a person is expected to carry out those duties.
- We should consider the processes of *training and providing replacements* for these individuals.
- We should consider how to show *recognition* for people's commitment and efforts, and *reward* their dedication, work and service to the parish.

The areas above are essential to the support and support systems we will explore in this chapter and are one route onto the sort of virtuous spiral (see Figure 6.1) which can help people realize their full potential in the life of the parish. This spiral should be a natural process which draws people in, involves them in parish life, supports and cares for them, teaches and guides them, and rewards their efforts.

We could start anywhere on the virtuous spiral but we have chosen to begin by exploring pastoral care.

Figure 6.1. Virtuous spiral of involvement.

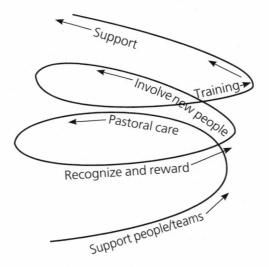

Pastoral care

There are a number of support systems in place for priests and pastors within the community and within different church organizations; however, these are designed for particular aspects of the work that the priest or pastor does. They include spiritual guidance, professional exchange across parishes and between denominations, and some mentoring.

Alongside this, the priest or pastor will find that they are encouraged to build relationships with others to help them as they carry out their roles within the parish. An established priest or pastor will have a range of people (mainly outside the parish) who make up their informal support network. Members of the priest's or pastor's own family may also be available as part of that support system and, in the case of the Anglican Church, there may be a spouse and children there to provide some of that support, too. These support systems can help the priest or pastor through difficult periods and assist them (indirectly) in their work, making decisions and carrying out their often difficult role.

Alongside these official, semi-official and informal sources of support, the parish has a duty to take care of its officers, just as the officers have a duty to serve the parish.

Naturally, the priest or pastor is not the only person that the parish needs to be thinking about providing care and support to. The question is, what can the parish do to ensure that care and support are provided for those who serve the parish?

Continuing with the example of the priest or pastor we can see that in the Catholic Church the Pastoral Parish Council or its equivalent has sometimes considered itself responsible for some of the pastoral care of the priest. They may try to ensure that the burdens placed on the priest are reasonable and that support is always there when problems arise. Of course, not all Catholic parishes have such councils and many of those that exist have either been set up without this area as part of their duties or feel that such ideas are presumptuous, inappropriate or not possible. The nature and tradition of each Council will determine how feasible such a role is for their situation.

Commitment to the care of the priest can be found in Church of England PCCs as they are committed to work in partnership with the priest, and this partnership extends into a keen interest in the performance and welfare of their priest.

Despite all of this, it is difficult to find any evidence of specific groups or individuals being officially assigned by the parish to support and provide pastoral care to the parish priest. Furthermore, it is not easy to find evidence of clergy seeking out and building a support team for themselves. The range of reactions to suggesting such an idea in parishes frequently produces responses such as, 'Why would you want to do that?', 'Is that an appropriate thing to do?', 'Isn't that the bishop's job?', 'Priests have enough support already, don't they?' and 'We've never had one before'. These comments can be answered as follows:

- *Why do that?* Most of the priests who 'burn out' through overwork and stress displayed all of the symptoms of their predicament months before the condition became critical, but the existing systems failed to note these symptoms and did nothing. This was mainly because the symptoms were more obvious to those the priest worked alongside than they were to external bodies and groups. A small parish-based support team concerned with the pastoral care of the priest could have made a significant difference in many of these cases.
- *Are they appropriate?* There is a variety of different ways in which such support teams can be developed. They need to be sensitive in a number of ways. For example, such teams would be inappropriate if they worked to promote the interests of the clergy above those of the parish (they are not the priest's 'fan club'!). They should not be in place of any pastoral care provided by the diocese or other church structures and would not have authority over the priest (not be their 'minders'). They should not assume or accept authority with regard to the management or leadership of the parish (not be 'back door managers').
- *Priests already have enough support.* The issue is often not about how much support is available but where it is available and what sort of support it is. Should all of the pastoral care of a parish priest lie outside the boundaries of the parish? Can this result in an 'us and them' situation between the parish and the clergy and hierarchy? Does the parish have no responsibility for its priest? Such teams should not take over existing roles and should provide as much or as little support as is needed.
- *Never had it before.* This is an argument against change, regardless of the nature of the change. Is such an argument more powerful than 'I wish we had done something sooner', 'Why did we let this get to this stage?'?

Putting together pastoral care teams

People usually have four questions about pastoral care teams. First, they want to know who should be in such a team. Next, they want to know how such teams are chosen and brought together and change over time. Third, they want to know how they operate and what their remit is. Finally, they want to know how they fit in with other aspects of parish and diocesan life.

Who should be in pastoral care teams?

Teams can be made up of a number of different types of members. It may include particular officers in the parish alongside a local doctor and a teacher as well as ordinary parish members. The team needs to be balanced, with different views available and with different aspects of concern present. It should be a confidential group without usurping the position of the priest's confessor. So the people need to be mature and competent, experienced and caring, with a wish to provide some degree of support and care to their clergy in order to ensure that they do their job well without either damaging themselves or those around them through overwork, stress, isolation.

How can pastoral care teams be chosen, brought together and change over time?

One way is for the PCC or Pastoral Council to form such a group or for them to invite someone (e.g. a past chair or similar) to do this. Alternatively, the priest might ask the Council to work with him or her to form a team. In each case the idea is to select a small (maximum six) team who can meet together with (and sometimes without) the priest to informally discuss relevant matters and offer themselves as an informal but confidential sounding board for the priest. Team members should not be 'yes' men. Indeed, the team will not work properly or may have a seriously detrimental effect on the parish if this is the case. There needs to be mutual respect between the team and the priest. Support does not exclude honest and frank exchanges. The team should agree a maximum time for membership and should keep to that rule.

How do they operate, and what is their remit?

The team should have a regular time to meet with the priest. A lunch or dinner is often good as long as enough time is made available. The meetings will be determined by the needs of the priest, by the level of activity and nature of the parish, the personalities involved and the concerns that currently exist in the team, priest and parish. In some cases a quarterly meeting might be enough and in other cases there might be periods of much more regular meetings. The team will aim to discuss parish, pastoral and personal matters with their priest and offer themselves as an informal but confidential sounding board. They will discuss the kinds of pressures the priest is facing and how he or she is coping, perhaps even talk about ideas such as training, extra clerical or other support before the priest takes these matters up with the parish or the diocese. They will be a safety valve and an early warning system, and a source of safe, trustworthy friendships.

How do pastoral care teams fit in with other aspects of parish and diocesan life?

In simple terms, a stable and productive priest is good news for both the parish and the diocese. At a more focused level, the parish is a community made up of members of God's family, and every member of the family is precious. The kinds of pressures and expectations placed on people like the priest make them vulnerable members of our community, and it is as much the duty of the parish to care for their priest as it is for the priest to care for the parish.

Pastoral care: general principles

What we learn from considering the pastoral care team concept is that the parish needs to think very carefully about how it cares for its members. It may be the case that we need to look at other people within our parish team and plan to provide them with similar forms of support. It may be that to have a team to look after everyone is a flight of fancy but it might help us see where alternatives could work. Thus, members of the Parish Council and other groups might consider adopting the idea of a 'buddying' system where every new member is assigned a 'buddy' to help them through the induction process and act as a mentor for them as they develop their skills in the role of Council member.

Pastoral care exists within most groups to some extent, but if we are to develop that aspect of the group we need to build the relationships within the group and develop it. Attending meetings may not be enough, in itself, to develop relationships within a group or team. The buddy system can help address this problem. So can having an annual 'away day' or even a weekend away. Groups can also plan to have a Christmas meal together or a social event such as a barbeque in the summer or a special trip to the theatre, a concert or some other event or place.

This should not apply exclusively to the Parish and other Councils or groups that have regular meetings. We need to be aware that some teams within the parish only ever get together to carry out their duties and never meet together as a team in other circumstances. Parishes should seriously consider how they can address this issue in the context of pastoral care. Outings, meals, socials and other activities can be organized by specific groups or can also be organized to bring together several groups. Such activities are at the heart of team building and go together with other forms of affirming actions to help make the teams and the parish stronger and happier.

Timing and care

The constitutions of clubs, charities and many Councils contain clauses which specify the length of time someone is allowed to remain as an officer or a member. The time element is seen as important for all kinds of good reasons (keeping the group fresh, avoiding burn-out and so on). These good reasons are also relevant to other activities within the parish.

The timing for roles and regular tasks within the parish may not be appropriate or practical in every case. However, the parish should consider developing a process whereby all roles and tasks are held under review and are monitored in order to ensure that no one ends up being trapped in a particular role or ends up claiming a role to the detriment of the parish as a whole.

Training and providing replacements

Training and finding replacements for people in different roles is a very important aspect of pastoral care. Training may not entail a huge amount of work or take a great deal of time, but even the simplest of things, if not explained, can cause major embarrassment or difficulties. As a simple example, consider the difference between seeing something taking place every Sunday and actually taking part in making that thing happen. Seeing it take place does not provide you with significant little details ('Where is the key for this cabinet kept?', 'Where do the books come from?', 'What order do we do this in?', 'Do I go first or follow?'). No one should be left to make a mistake in front of the parish.

People in existing roles build on their knowledge through training, while people new to the role have training as part of the introductory process. Before taking on a new role each person needs to become familiar and comfortable with the role. New recruits usually start by working as part of a team and then gradually take on more responsibility as they build confidence and experience. Finding replacements should be part of that gradual process where people are supported and nurtured into roles rather than 'thrown in at the deep end'.

Recognition and rewards

If the parish is served well by an individual or group, the parish needs to make strong efforts to recognize that service. Such recognition should not be an afterthought and neither should it simply be the equivalent of an official 'nod'. Recognition tends to operate on a public and a personal level, and so people who are given recognition should be afforded it in the eyes of the parish (at a service, in the newsletter) and privately by the key senior members of the community whose recognition would be appreciated by the individual or group in question.

Rewards for service can come in a variety of ways and may simply be proper thanks but can also be given in more creative ways (through public presentations of gifts, etc.) and in official ways such as the awarding of an honorary position or some similar action (for example, some parishes may be able to arrange recognition from the bishop or the awarding of a medal or honour from within a society or church body).

All of this leads us on to the other two themes of this chapter: involving people and building teams.

How do people get involved?

For many who have little or no involvement in the life and work of the parish it may seem that there is a type of person who gets involved in the parish. Often they cannot imagine themselves in such a role because they feel they are not the kind of person the parish is looking for. Naturally, many of those currently deeply involved in parish life thought similar things before they became involved and some may still feel that way despite their involvement.

Examining how people become involved will help us develop a better approach to this important area.

The pyramid of involvement

In business there are a number of standard models illustrating how people become involved in products or services. A similar model applies in the parish context. Figure 6.2 illustrates the stages, from no involvement to a high degree of engagement with the life of the parish. It is not designed to be a hierarchy in the sense of one level being more important than another but rather to indicate the differences in degrees of involvement usually experienced. We must remember that not everyone who becomes involved at one level will want or be able to increase their involvement. Additionally, we may find that some people become very heavily involved in a number of different activities all at the same level, resulting in a considerable contribution to parish life.

With these caveats in place, we can still see that one of the key ways of recruiting people for roles further up the pyramid is by recruiting them onto the first level.

Figure 6.2. The pyramid of involvement.

Once a person has built enough confidence as an *ad hoc* or casual helper in a parish activity or role they will be more inclined (and more confident) to become a member of the team carrying out that role on a regular basis. The opportunity is there to build on their growing experience by offering them some training or more formal guidance in the role. This can lead to them becoming a full member of the team or rota for that activity and their experience will allow them to both take on responsibility and feel confident that this is something they can do. By becoming part of the team they will become more formally part of the management process. They will have already been contributing to the running or routine maintenance of the role or activity, but as they gain in confidence and experience they will be more active in this area and will be more willing to assist in the supporting and training of newer members as well as assisting in the updating of rotas and the like.

Running or sharing in the running of the activity will no longer be as daunting as it had once been, and representing the group in meetings, on committees and so on may also be the next step for some. For a smaller number, this may be a route to discovering the calling to other, more demanding or authoritative roles within the parish.

One of the simple indicators which can be observed when examining how your parish's pyramid of involvement works is the number of people present at each level. If there is a large body of people present in the 'not involved' base and very few in the helping out and assisting sections your parish may be facing (or about to face) major problems. Parishes need a good-sized pool of willing and semi-involved people in order to make the whole system work.

One of the basic tasks of the parish is to build, maintain and keep nurturing people as they begin to become involved in parish life. Each small, casual exchange or encounter is really a door of opportunity opening. It is a signal that the person is open to greater involvement, and ignoring this sign is like denying a person the opportunity to become more committed to God. Every member of the parish has responsibility in this area, as the door may not be opened to the priest or even the person or team leading the activity.

So, how do people move into the first level of involvement?

The involvement catalysts

A catalyst is something which causes something else to happen. A catalyst can be very closely linked to the change it causes or it can be not obviously related to the change itself. The list below illustrates how different these catalysts are. The most common catalysts which take people from a position where they are not involved or engaged with parish life and involves them are as follows.

- *Chance, or a random event.* Being in a certain place at a certain time may mean that the person is asked to do something completely 'out of the blue'. For example, they may be asked to help stack chairs or hold something for someone or assist in bringing a disabled person to the front of the church and so on. This action can bring the person to the attention of a member of the team, can reveal aspects of the value of that activity to the person, and can be an introduction which results in the person being asked again.
- *Helping a friend out.* This is very similar to the 'chance event' above.
- *Partner involved.* Many people end up becoming involved because their husband, wife, boy- or girlfriend is involved.
- *Child involvement.* Children are often involved in a number of different aspects of the parish. Parents take and collect children, sit with children during events, take part in the events in order to ensure that they happen, become involved in order to encourage their children to take part. Having children is one of the strongest catalysts.
- *Attending a meeting.* There are a number of public meetings which non-involved parish members can attend (the parish AGM is a good example). Once there, the person can either be involved through some random event (as above) or by having their interest or concern sparked by events at the meeting. Those who speak at meetings can expect to be approached at some stage after.
- *Pulpit recruitment.* Any number of appeals take place during the year as the priest or another person stands up before the congregation and asks for volunteers or willing helpers.
- *Notices/posters/newsletters.* All these serve to bring opportunities to people's notice and can encourage people to open up and offer their help.
- *Social functions.* As with meetings and chance events, attending a social function can lead to greater involvement in parish life.
- *Personal approach.* People become involved because other people ask them to do something. This can be as described above (random). It can be more involved and related to the person's particular skills (an accountant, social worker, architect, etc.) or through recommendations or reputation. Whatever the cause, personal approaches are at the heart of recruitment.

- *Desire to become involved.* This is a simple and obvious case. The person may want to do whatever role or activity within the parish appeals to them.
- *Changes in personal life.* People's lives change, their children grow up and leave home, they become widowed, they retire or are made redundant. Changes in a person's life may lead them to become available for different roles and activities and may cause them to wish to become more involved.
- *Events and experiences.* Major events, and sometimes minor ones, can influence people and change their lives. Terrorist activities, natural disasters, personal tragedies can all cause people to re-examine their lives. This can lead to a desire to become more involved in some aspect of parish life.

It is perhaps not surprising but it is very instructive to realize that the more active a parish becomes, the more opportunities it creates for its members to become involved in parish life and the greater the number of catalysts arise. It is also important to note that people seldom become involved as a result of one single catalyst. Sometimes the process is very gradual and is the result of a combination of feelings and different signals or encounters. The greater the involvement, the longer the process may be.

Once people have decided to become part of a group or take on a particular role within the parish, it becomes necessary to consider how the parish makes best use of these people. We have already looked at care and at motivation. Now we turn our attention to the concept of teams and how they work.

Involvement and team building

One of the enduring themes of this book is that the parish is a community made up of the family of God. When we talk about involvement, we stress how this is a way in which we can develop our potential within the community and family. So, when we examine teams within the parish we are not looking at groups that are set apart from or are added on alongside the community. They are of and from and within the parish, working with and serving the parish's needs. A team that looks at the rest of the parish and feels the need to think in 'us and them' terms has problems and may become a problem for the parish.

Parishes tend to have a number of different types of teams which include those that:

- *are official parts of the structure of the parish*, such as the PCC; these teams are a permanent part of the parish as a whole but they need to be nurtured and developed, as do all other teams.
- *run or organize particular things*. They make social events, catechetical groups and the like happen. They are tasked with putting together the elements of the event, club or set of meetings and find people to help them carry out the task. They tend to have a formal structure and hold regular meetings which may become more frequent during the period leading up to the next event or session they are planning. They usually exist as permanent teams with a rolling membership of people.
- *carry out functions, tasks or roles*. Most typically, these are teams who provide the parish with a service on a regular basis. They might represent the people who do the cleaning or flower arranging, the welcoming or the tea after the main Sunday service. They may have an even more liturgical or spiritual role such as providing the music or organizing the choir, or perhaps planning the provision of readers and so on. This type of team may not operate with a formal committee-style structure and in some cases may not gather together as a whole group on any regular or formal basis at all, but might be a set of small groups who share the task of providing a particular service.
- *are brought together on an* ad hoc *basis*. Some teams within a parish are set up to carry out a particular 'one-off' task such as repairing the roof, rebuilding the hall, running a special disaster appeal and such things. Although formal in structure and assigned authority and priority within the parish, they tend to be temporary and specialized groups.
- *part of or linked to other structures based outside the parish*. These

95

can be groups linked with the diocese or the national church such as those concerned with justice and peace, Mothers' Union, Women's Institute, Fair Trade and so on, or linked with particular charities, organizing Alpha or Café courses or be part of pressure groups or religious orders such as the Franciscans, Iona Community and the like. Despite connections with outside bodies, such teams will act within the context of being an integral part of the parish.

Working in even the simplest team structure acts as a binding agent, bringing the individuals together as a team. A lot of research has gone into looking at how this natural binding process works, and we can identify basic elements in that process which we can work on to ensure that teams get on together and produce better outcomes for all concerned. The main elements are:

- *Spending time together*. This builds relationships and supports the growth of the group as a team. Building in social and other time together ensures that teams grow and work better together.
- *Improving communications*. Information exchange prevents problems, solves disputes, builds trust, improves effectiveness. Elements such as rules or procedures need to be sensitively and effectively communicated and kept up to date to avoid confusion.
- *Respect and tolerance*. Complacency and ignorance in this area may lead to unintentional problems. Vigilance, care and sensitivity go together well with equality and diversity and should help prevent most problems.
- *Building trust*. The first three aspects of team building help build trust, as does openness and honesty across the group. The acts of giving and accepting criticism are better achieved in an atmosphere of trust, and if we want to improve the way we do things as a team and learn how to serve our parish better, we need to build trust within our team. Trust also helps teams survive through difficult times.
- *Personal and group development*. Not every team requires highly developed skills or knowledge. Not every team needs to develop routines or actions based on highly polished co-ordination. But every team is made up of people who can be supported and devel-

oped both in their role and as individuals. Team membership could allow the parish the opportunity to offer them development in other areas beyond their current role.

Conclusions

We have used the idea of a virtuous spiral to illustrate how the act of caring for and supporting individuals and teams within the parish can build into a process where people's efforts are cherished and rewarded and where this can flow into a process of attracting more people into the life and work of the parish. Of course this process works both as a spiral, drawing people in and helping people grow, and also as a range of actions and approaches to the life of the parish which exist in parallel with each other. In other words, attracting new people will be happening at the same time as people are being trained, supported and cared for, rewarded and so on. They are facets of parish life as well as stages in a living process.

The principles explored and illustrated in this chapter can be applied across the whole range of parish activities. In the next chapter we will look at how we deal with communications in relation to different aspects of parish life, and explore in more detail how these are managed.

7

How the Parish Meets and Communicates

All of them were filled with the Holy Spirit and began to speak in other tongues, as the Spirit enabled them.

Acts 2.4

Introduction

In the professional world there is a wide range of different models of what communication is and how communication works in different circumstances. We will look at how to identify and assess the existing channels of communication within the parish and explore how we can develop and improve parish communications with clear and sensible aims in mind.

Elements of communication

What are the important factors determining the quality of any communication? A great deal of work has been done in this area by academics and commercial organizations but the basics remain the same. To consider any communication we have to look at the following factors.

- *The message content.* What does the message contain, what are its details?
- *The message's value.* How powerful, meaningful, relevant, enlightening will it be? What is its authority and where does that come from?
- *The message's quality.* How well is the message put together and presented? How well does it say what it intends to say?
- *The targeting of the message.* Is it aimed at the people it should be, and is it reaching those people?

- *The medium carrying the message.* How is the message reaching the people it is aimed at? How effective is that medium at putting across your message, reaching your intended audience, and how well do they receive the message via that medium?
- *Interference affecting the message.* What will affect the way in which your message will be received by your audience? How is it affecting the communication process (distorting the message, affecting the medium, interfering with the ability of the listener to hear and understand, etc.)?
- *The recipient of the message.* The circumstances of each recipient will affect how they receive and react to the message.
- *Response and feedback.* Communication is essentially a two-way process, so as you communicate (or soon after communicating) the message you will need to be monitoring how the message is being received, what the reactions are to the message, and be prepared to answer the reactions or response you receive with your own feedback.

These factors are all part of what is known as the classical model of communication. Figure 7.1 illustrates this. The simple explanation is that the sender 'encodes' the message. The sender's ability to encode will depend on the content of the message, the abilities and frame of mind of the sender and the assumptions made by the sender about the people the message is intended for. The message is carried by the

Figure 7.1. The classic communication model.

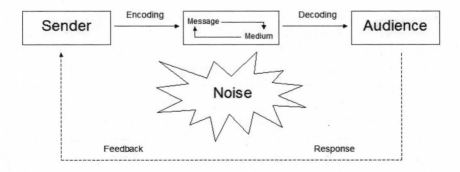

medium. This medium may carry many other messages at the same time (think of a newspaper for example) and these will vary in type and value including advice, news, information, advertising and so on. Much of this will be background interference or 'noise'.

The intended recipient or audience will have to make sense of or 'decode' the message, and the capacity to do that will depend on the abilities and circumstances of the audience and on what is called the 'signal-to-noise ratio' which is a simple measure of how much noise the receiver needs to deal with in order to find the message. The greater the noise compared to the message, the harder it will be. Then comes the possibility that the audience has received and decoded the message and that they react to it (positively, negatively, etc.) and do something as a result (answer, smile, buy, etc.). The sender has to be able to listen out for that reaction or feedback and be ready to respond to it. The process becomes a cycle as communication causes responses which cause the sender to answer with their own communication.

Although this may seem somewhat removed from the communication process experienced by the ordinary person, it is only a model which breaks down what happens in everyday life. For example, we can describe a phone call using this model.

Person A is the sender. Person B is her friend. A has personal problems at home and does not feel able to go out. She has analysed her situation, decided she cannot go out, sorts out what she will say to B and calls her on the phone. B answers and A says who she is, that she cannot go and briefly explains why. B argues, not being able to see how upset A really is and feeling upset herself as she really wants to go out. A gives her more information and begins to reveal how upset she really is. B responds sympathetically and A releases her emotions. They decide not to go to the cinema but B will visit A and they will have a meal together instead.

Using the model, we can see how the message was encoded, how the message and the medium combined to create noise, how additional noise came from the audience (Person B), and how the decoding was affected. We can see how the response creates a feedback in A, who modifies her message which is easier to decode and creates more response and more feedback, and so on.

This kind of model is a useful descriptive tool, giving us insight into what is happening within the communications process. It is also a tool which helps us assess, identify problem areas and improve communications.

Communications within the parish

Each parish community will enjoy its own little idiosyncrasies. The normal way to inform parishioners in one parish will be the wrong way in another. However, the vast majority of types of communication can be listed and explored without too much difficulty. We have listed the majority below (Figure 7.2).

Examine the list and create your own note of how communication works within your parish and alongside the communication channels try listing the major uses that each are put to. You can do this yourself or work together with other members of the parish who are interested in this area.

Figure 7.2. Chart of communications channels within a parish.

Communication channels	General applications	Audiences
Face to face – formal	Personal formal, worship, business and management, committees, meetings of all kinds, structured or authority situations, etc.	Any individuals, groups, colleagues, staff, senior members of church, etc.
Face to face – informal	Personal but informal: most situations.	Any individuals or groups.
Telephone – formal	Personal formal, worship, business and management, committees, structured or authority situations, etc.	Individuals, unlikely to communicate with groups in this way.

Communication channels	General applications	Audiences
Telephone – informal	Personal but informal to individuals.	Any individual.
E-mail	Formal/informal, personal/general, computer or web-linked exchanges, etc.	Any individual and some groups.
Memos/written notes	Mainly formal (memos), informal (notes), some replaced by e-mail.	Usually those associated with aspects of life of church.
Letters	Mainly formal, some may be personal, most official or business.	Usually individuals but some groups.
Leaflets	General information, announcements, publicity, etc.	Groups targeted by method of distribution.
Announcements	Usually public or to groups, mainly formal, information, comments, etc.	Congregations, groups, gatherings, meetings, etc.
Notice boards – public in church, hall, etc.	Announcements, publicity, advice, information, etc.	Directed to all using the space where board is located.
Notice boards – public in non-church locations	Announcements, publicity, advice, information displayed in libraries, schools, etc.	Aimed at those not normally using church or hall.
Notice boards – in office locations	Announcements, publicity, advice, information, etc.	Narrow audience of staff, volunteers, etc.
Websites	Announcements, publicity, advice, information, evangelism, etc.	Parishioners and non-parishioners, usually open access.
Newsletters	News, announcements, reflections, etc.	Usually parishioners and visitors.

Communication channels	General applications	Audiences
Magazines	Entertainment, news, announcements, reflections, community/ parish life, etc.	Parishioners and local population.
Other church publications	Announcements, news, reflection and debate.	Readers/viewers and parishioners, etc.
Non-church media	Advertising, announcements, news, reflection and debate.	All who use the medium in question.
Gossip and rumour	Informal, difficult to control, often destructive or unhelpful.	Members/non-members of parish.
Other		

Once you have built a full picture of the communications in your parish try to answer the following questions regarding each that you have identified. Ask for each:

- What sort of format or communication types are employed in the channel? (Communication formats)
- How does it work? How does information flow across the channel? (Distribution/flow)
- Who would you say are the primary individuals or groups responsible for the messages communicated through each channel? (Originators)
- What kinds of information types are using these channels? (Information types)
- Is the information flowing one way or is it a channel of information exchange? (Direction of flow)
- How open or restricted is the information flow within your parish? (Level of restriction)
- Who would you say controls the key aspects of this flow? (Control)
- What purposes are served by this communications channel? (Purpose)

- Which groups/individuals are served by this communications channel? (Who does it serve?)
- On a scale of one to five, where one is very good and five is very poor, give the group's (or your own) assessment of the effectiveness of each communications channel within your parish. (Effectiveness)

This assessment will provide you with the basic picture of information flows and channels of communication within your parish alongside a simple (subjective) measure of their effectiveness. Where do you go from here?

Examining why you have given each channel a particular score will help the group understand what it expects from each channel. This should help you understand each channel better and will lead to good ideas on how to improve communications.

Five key points to remember when improving communications are:

1. Understand your audience and tailor your message and select your medium accordingly.
2. Reduce 'noise' by using each medium appropriately, by avoiding conflicting messages and by keeping language simple and clear.
3. Provide clear channels for response.
4. Answer comments and enquiries immediately.
5. Keep information up to date. Essential for websites, notice boards, newsletters and all regular communications.

Meetings

Parish life is full of meetings, from the very largest of gatherings to small, intimate meetings. Here we aim to help you to make major improvements to all of the meetings in your parish.

Managing a parish is about getting people to work together and about everyone who takes part feeling that they have contributed. This can be achieved when you run positive and effective meetings.

So, let us start by looking at what sort of meetings parishes tend to have. We will not include the specifically spiritually-based meetings but we should keep in mind that every meeting held within the context of the parish has a spiritual aspect to it and has Christ at its centre. Prayers and reflection should be an integral element in all meetings held within or on behalf of the parish.

Meetings come in a variety of sizes:

Very large meetings

These are gatherings such as the Annual General Meetings held for the whole parish and other extraordinary meetings where major decisions are discussed or announced or where the parish needs to be consulted as a whole. They are characterized by a division between those who have called and are running the meeting and the main body of people who attend the meeting. There will usually be some sort of convener or chair who will lead the meeting, there may be a panel of other people alongside this person and there may be some kind of presentation to the body of people attending. Very limited individual involvement and contributions are possible from the floor during these meetings. These meetings are either infrequent (once a year or less) or *ad hoc* in nature.

Large meetings

Smaller than the whole parish but still large enough for a hall. Similar in style, but scale of decisions not as great with a more focused group of people attending. May be more regular (more than once a year) or part of a series, although some will be *ad hoc*.

Medium-sized meetings

These come in a variety of forms, may not require the main hall and could be an 'open' session of a committee or Council meeting. Some committee or Council meetings may be of a size that they can be classed in this category. Depending on the purpose of the meeting, there may be exchange and involvement from the floor. These tend to be more regular (quarterly, for example) or part of a series where progress is being reported back or where discussion is linked with periods of action, reflection or discussion.

Small meetings

Narrow and specifically limited membership, agendas, scope and outcomes. All those invited tend to be members of the meeting and attend on a regular basis, and all take part in the meeting. They are regular and dates are agreed several meetings in advance. Members may represent a larger group's interests at the meeting or may have been elected or in some other way appointed.

Mini-meetings

Either meetings formed from sub-groups of other meetings or business meetings necessary for the more day-to-day running of the parish or small group. They are not open and conduct specific pieces of business, are limited to relevant individuals and tend to be less formal than the others, although still professionally conducted. They can also be *ad hoc*, informal meetings and specialized.

Meetings also come in a variety of formats. Some of the more common examples are illustrated in Figure 7.3 and are briefly described below.

Formal public meetings

Illustrated in (a), where a stage, platform or front of the hall is laid out for a chairperson, other speakers and/or panel and the body of attendees face them as for an audience. Much of the business of the meeting is conducted from the chair or platform.

Less formal large gatherings

Illustrated in formats (a), (b) and sometimes (d), these range from events such as speakers' events through to public debates and discussions. Although the proceedings may be well scheduled and the event controlled through its format and by ushers, the structure may have no legal or official status requiring it to operate in specific ways.

'Fishbowl'-style meetings

Typically layouts (b) or (c), a common way of providing public or semi-public access to more formal meetings. For example, if a committee or Parish Council wants to involve the parish in its decision-making and show how it goes about its business, it can invite people to observe an ordinary meeting. It can do this by either rotating invitations around small groups of representatives or they can hold a meeting in the hall and invite people to observe the proceedings.

Consultative meetings

Typically (a), (b) or (c) but variations as below, too. Some are large public meetings and some smaller, more focused meetings where, for example, representatives of different groups within the parish participate. These may be better managed, with a layout which breaks down barriers between the different groups.

Consulting/discussion and exploratory meetings

Typically (d), (e) or (f) in layout, these can be consultative (as above) or where social or religious education and training take place. They may include speakers and audio-visual elements and allow the larger body to split into smaller groups for discussion/exchanges of views.

Less formal medium-sized meetings

These can vary in format but can be a less formal, smaller-scale version of (b) or (c) as illustrated in (j) or perhaps even (f) or (g) where catering is seen as part of the proceedings. Social interaction is often an important part of this type of meeting.

Committees and councils

Formal business-focused meetings with limited membership and where layout and proceedings are designed to enable the most efficient exchange of views and speedy progress through, often difficult, committee work. Typically in a smaller space than a hall and with simple layouts such as (h) or (i) although may be 'in the round' such as in (j).

Smaller meetings

These are designed for specific purposes throughout the life of the parish and may take place in rooms or even in the hall. Their format will be determined by the business they have to carry out and can be formally laid out as in (f), more open format as in (j) although even small groups sometimes end up splitting up and doing team tasks as in (k) or (l).

It is clear from this brief outline that meetings can take on a number of different roles, styles and formats and can affect parish life in a variety of ways. Here is a list of the major reasons why your parish might hold a meeting of some or all of its members. No doubt, on reflection you will find other reasons to add to this list:

- *Statutory reasons*. The parish is required to hold specific meetings in order to function as a parish (the AGM, Council meetings and the like may be included in this).
- *Informing the parish*. When key decisions have been made; when problems affecting all or part of the parish arise; when decisions need to be passed on from the diocese or higher up the hierarchy to the parish, etc.
- *Seeking advice*. When issues arise that require consultation of some form from members of the parish as a whole or sub-sets of the parish.
- *Solving problems*. It may be necessary to resolve issues, solve problems or bring the whole parish together to reach the solution to a problem affecting the parish as a whole (or a sub-set of it).

Figure 7.3. Examples of meeting layouts and styles.

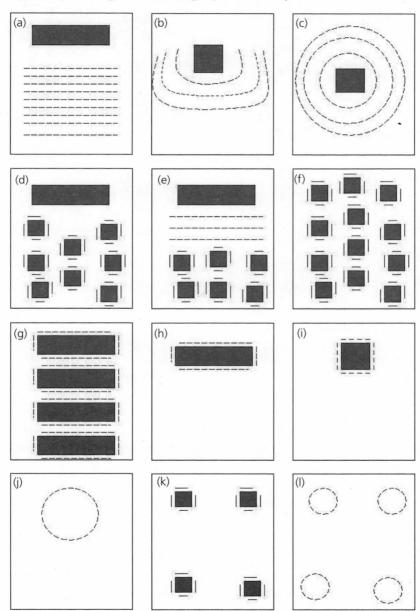

- *Clarification meetings.* Sometimes it is important to reach more than just a consensus, the parish may need to gain a much clearer understanding of an issue or concern and this may be best dealt with in one or more meetings.
- *Information exchange.* Not all meetings are where decisions need to take place. They are also opportunities to learn, share, teach, discuss.
- *Decision-making.* Coming together to decide how the parish wants to address a problem, solve a difficulty, or select the preferred option.
- *Completing business.* Many aspects of parish life require meetings in order for things to be done. These range from elections of officers and agreeing of accounts through to appointing contractors, selecting designs, agreeing project content and so on.
- *Recognition and rewarding.* Publicly recognizing individuals and groups is something that communities such as parishes should do and should be good at doing.
- *Celebrating.* Parishes need to celebrate together as well as work together on the day-to-day business issues. Celebrating and rewarding or recognizing achievement all contain basic elements of what makes a meeting work.
- *Sharing and support.* There may be times when this is necessary or desirable. We need to gather together at times of tragedy or celebration or at times when such events need to be remembered and create opportunities where we can share with and support each other.

We can also identify a number of situations where meetings will be inappropriate or unhelpful. Try to avoid meetings if what you aim to do is:

- Carry out detailed work.
- Discuss individuals and private or personal issues.
- Introduce highly controversial issues.
- Handle issues of very limited scope.
- Present items for discussion that have already been decided.
- Hold a meeting without any real purpose.

Once considered, there will be other situations where you believe that a meeting is not necessary. So, while we are examining the negative aspects of meetings, let us take this opportunity to clear out the bad practices and simple errors we have encountered so that we can get to the heart of what makes a good meeting. Again, feel free to add to the list. When meetings run into difficulties, the most commonly occurring problems are as follows:

- *Poorly defined or confused objectives or expectations*. Few people will be able to feel satisfied with the outcome of a meeting where the objectives and expectations are confused or deliberately obscured.
- *Roles and responsibilities not properly defined*. Either nothing gets done or people duplicate actions.
- *'Too many cooks' syndrome*. Again, duplication, confusion, no direction.
- *Confusion of purpose*. The meeting may be focused on a subject but some will be debating the importance of the topic, others the content of the topic and so on.
- *Questions of authority and power*. Get the remit, power and authority clear before the meeting.
- *Manipulation and abuse of power*. The leader or chair can subvert and control meetings. When meetings are there to 'rubber stamp' or pander to the views of its chair or leader, they are not useful, valid or morally justifiable.
- *Agenda highjacking*. People with their own agendas and those who wish to dominate groups with their own opinions can disrupt and damage meetings.
- *Personal attacks*. Meetings can sometimes be used to carry out personal vendettas. Alternatively, personality clashes may arise. Neither have a place in meetings.
- *Access to the debate*. A question of chairing the meeting. Let everyone have their say.
- *Communication breakdown*. It does not have to be complete breakdown. If people do not listen to each other, you eventually risk much greater levels of communication breakdown.
- *Personality clashes*. Even minor clashes can cause problems of tension

and result in a lack of openness and trust. Such feelings can breed distrust, cause friction, create cliques and lead to poor communication.

- *'Here we go again' syndrome.* Some meetings seem to go over and over the same ground, again and again. This can make them last longer, become tedious and less effective.
- *Information overload.* Too much detail can reduce effectiveness; too many detailed reports, figures and facts can constipate meetings.
- *Fuzzy decision-making.* If the meeting ends up compromising on virtually every issue encountered, if none of their decisions feels satisfactory or complete, the meetings will lose commitment and focus and will feel like a waste of time.
- *The habit of avoiding problems.* Some committees will have a member who does not want to address any real issues and will try to deny the existence of any real problems. This attitude can be infectious and can erode the usefulness of a meeting or committee.
- *Negativity rules.* Similar to the 'No problems here' person is the 'There is nothing we can do about it' person. As with problem avoidance, powerlessness can be used as a tool to ensure that you do not challenge anyone in authority.
- *Total lack of momentum.* It can be the case that the same items arise in the agenda of every meeting because no progress has been made with those items between meetings. Such problems can turn people away from and turn them against the meetings in question.
- *Problems with the meeting environment.* The venue can be the problem that's killing the meeting. Problems may be poor sightlines, difficulties in hearing people, bad lighting, bad environment, a lack of hospitality and care, etc.
- *Other related problems with the meeting.* The timing, location and signage relating to a meeting can be crucial to how people experience the event.
- *Bad meeting management.* In addition to everything so far, poor meetings often have poorly thought through and badly written agendas. They often have badly thought out content, frequently run out of time or greatly over-run as a result of poor or no time management.

Even after readers have added more problems to the list it is most likely that all of the difficulties faced can be addressed through the advice gathered together under the three following headings:

1. Be better prepared for your meetings.
2. Have more effective chairing of the meetings and better meetings behaviour.
3. Make sure you follow up each meeting properly.

We have already indicated that there can be a number of different types of meeting held within a parish. Where variations to advice are relevant we will flag them clearly. However, the advice is here to be used to help you improve your meetings, not hinder them with unnecessary rules. Remember, these lists are not exhaustive.

Preparing for a meeting

What do we need to do to prepare effectively for the meeting? The following elements are important when you are planning a new meeting, trying to rescue a failing meeting or want to keep a good meeting running.

Understand the purpose(s) of the meeting

Make sure that the meeting needs to take place before you start planning it. If the meeting is already established and necessary, make sure you are clear about what its purposes are. Perhaps the members of the meeting need to take time out to pray and reflect so that they can bring a fresher, more focused approach to the proceedings.

Meetings in a parish usually have two underlying goals – to serve the parish in a positive and loving manner, and to serve God. If all else fails when looking for positive or useful aspects to a meeting, start with these two goals and work back.

Work out who should attend the meeting

The meeting may have a standard set of attendees as defined by rules, laws or tradition. Who else should attend? Is there a need for occasional guest speakers? Is the mix right? How long have people been members?

Clarify who has what role within the meeting

Although meetings may appear to be straightforward, there can often be details that are left out of the planning and which cause problems every time the meeting is convened. Here are some roles to think about in your meetings:

- *Chair or equivalent.* The person whose responsibility it is to manage the meeting as a whole.
- *Organizer(s)/leader(s) of prayers and reflections.* Each meeting will usually require someone or a group who can provide this. It should be possible to rotate responsibility for this.
- *Person to take the minutes.* This can be rotated but the quality of minutes can have a major effect on the way the meeting works. Can all of the key members be trained in simple minute-taking? Do not impose the role on one person, do not make sexist assumptions and sort it out well before the meeting is convened.
- *Secretary.* This is not usually the minute-keeper but does the administration for the meetings – books the room or hall, sends out minutes and notices, chases up people, etc.
- *Time-keeper.* To help the chair keep things to time.
- *People to set up and clear the room.* Having a rota for these can make a big difference to some meetings.
- *Welcomers and hospitality providers.* Who is going to ensure that the newer members of the meeting are made welcome, who sorts out refreshments, etc.?
- *People responsible for items on the agenda.* To ensure all of the business gets done, make sure that key people attend (or agree items and issues with them if they can't be there).

- *Guests and observers.* These need to be flagged before the meeting starts along with their reasons for being at the meeting.
- *Facilitators and other specialists.* The meeting will dictate the need for any specialists.
- *Health and safety officer/first aid officer.* This person may not be required for the smaller meetings but should be considered as and when necessary.

The important thing to remember is that once you have agreed the roles you should have people primed and ready to take on these roles well before the meeting starts. Always endeavour to avoid roles being filled *ad hoc* at the beginning of a meeting.

Get the timing right

The timing is important. Everyone needs to know about the meeting well enough in advance to be sure that they can attend. In meetings where there are legal requirements regarding minimum length of time for issuing notice of the meeting you may decide that the minimum time is not enough. All major meetings can be in the parish calendar, they can be featured in the newsletters and magazines well before the time and flagged in posters before the 'official' announcements are made. For committees and similar groups, agree meetings several months in advance so that the next two or three can be in everyone's diaries.

Ad hoc or infrequent meetings need to be flagged effectively and all of those for whom the meeting is relevant need to be contacted well in advance (the secretary's job).

Perhaps you need to review the time of the meeting. When did you decide to have the meetings at that time? Is it still appropriate for the members? What problems does the time cause? Should it be changed? Sometimes changing the time of a meeting can transform attendance.

Be clear on how long the meeting should last and plan the meeting around that time slot. Leave time for arrivals and give people a reason to turn up early (refreshments?) so the meeting can start on time.

Get the location right

Think of the suitability of the venue, its location with regards to those you hope will attend, its appearance and ambiance, and what it will be like at the time of the meeting. What is it like on dark, cold and wet winter nights? Will it serve the purposes of the meeting or is it too small/large/inflexible? Can people park easily and is public transport convenient?

Develop the agenda for the meeting

Review the objectives of the meeting regularly and make sure the agenda is designed to meet those objectives. Meetings without formal or shared agendas still need clear plans. The advice given here is applicable to all forms of meetings. People with plans tend to get things done.

The agenda should be explicit about what the meeting needs to achieve. So, when you complete the agenda the meeting should have achieved all of its goals (or moved them on as required). For each individual agenda item, try to clearly identify and specify:

- *Who the 'owner' of the item is.* Who should be responsible for that item in the meeting?
- *What the purpose of the item is.* Is it an item that requires a decision (and what sort of decision will it need?) or is it information for the meeting?
- *What sort of discussion do you expect*? Consider the accompanying notes or report, ask yourself who will take an interest, who will take issue and so on.
- *How long will this item take*? The variables above will help, but it will be up to the chair to decide timings. Remember to allow for decisions and summarizing when estimating times.
- *Which order should the items follow*? In many meetings there are basic elements which always occur in the same sequence. However, when planning the agenda you need to be sensitive to how the meeting will deal with each item. Some useful suggestions are that you

might begin and end the meeting with items that you feel confident will be easy to handle or less contentious. Good news can be timed if the meeting requires such help. Make sure that items that need to follow on from each other actually do and that you keep apart items you expect to conflict with each other. Review the whole agenda against your target times for each item and consider how you might regain time if something over-runs. If a certain key player cannot stay beyond a certain time, cover their item earlier.

- *The basic agenda template.* Classically, meetings start with a welcome and apologies followed by an opening prayer or reflection. The minutes of the previous meeting are then reviewed, amended, agreed and signed off. Matters arising from the minutes not included in the agenda may be covered before the main business starts. At the end of the meeting there is usually a section for any other business (either sent to the chair before the meeting or offered at the start of the meeting). Dates of future meetings are reviewed and agreed before the closing prayer or reflection.

- *Keep it short and simple.* The agenda and the business of the meeting usually benefits from this simple aim (also known as KISS). However, do not let the desire to get through the business cause you to deny or truncate important discussions. Note that the papers sent out with the agenda, minutes, etc., will help determine how items are likely to be approached by the meeting. If an item requires discussion but the papers accompanying the item seem to leave little room for or expectation of any discussion, the chair needs to ask whether they should introduce the item in such a way that discussion is generated. Other items that seem to welcome discussion may not be worthy of as much time and may be cut short to make room for more important debates.

- *Build in time for 'comfort breaks'.* Consider the whole of the meeting and identify a possible point in the proceedings where people can stop for a few minutes.

- *Avoid unnecessary items and individual 'hobby horses'.* Be aware of the agendas of particular members and prepare to cut short unnecessary diversions during discussions. The majority of the meeting will support the curtailing of such diversions. Remember that the 'Any other business' part of the meeting should be kept for exceptional and important items. The most essential items can be covered first and less pressing items may be shunted to the next meeting.

• *Always build in arrival and departure elements to the front and back of the meeting.* Settling down and leaving can take time.

Making it happen

Successful meetings of all kinds have a checklist attached to them covering all of the things that need to be done before, during and after the meeting. People move on but the list remains. The items included in such a list are:

• *Being clear about the time and location.* Keep this up to date.
• *Booking the venue.* Book as far in advance as is practical, confirm nearer the time and then check again the week before.
• *Sort all of the technical details.* Do not leave this to the last minute. Check everything you can.
• *Be clear of the layout, seating and other special needs.* Make sure you know the space, are clear of what you want to do with it and that what you get is what you need.
• *Support people.* Everyone should know what they are doing, be confident of what others are doing and be happy in their roles.
• *Assemble all other materials.* Do you have enough paper, pens, glasses and jugs, coffee, tea and biscuits?
• *Control issues.* Whatever the control and security issues are, they need to be checked and managed. How will people be able to enter the building and who should be there to manage this?
• *Access, health, safety and other issues.* Have you and your team checked all of the relevant issues relating to these? When in doubt, check with the relevant person responsible in the parish or diocese.

Effective chairing of the meetings and better meetings behaviour

The main body of the meeting will rely on those in charge managing the process to make the ground rules clear at the beginning and whenever appropriate. The following notes and guidelines are aimed at those who end up being responsible for the running of the meeting. Teams need to agree roles and ground rules well before the meeting begins. Ideally, the ground rules should be so obvious and so fair that no one will be surprised or think of questioning them and no one will feel restricted by them.

These are the key elements that make meetings successful.

Start well

The beginning of the meeting usually signposts how the rest of the meeting will go. Aim to make a good start to the meeting. Try to start the meeting on time, so build in time for arriving and settling down, signal that it is about to start, avoid false starts and do not let late entries distract you. Let people know what is going to happen.

Don't forget introductions

Make sure people are properly introduced and introduce each section as it is reached. Keep the process clear, and keep using people's names and roles so that everyone knows what is going on and who is doing what.

Don't be afraid to re-state the meeting's objectives

Do this at the beginning when introducing the agenda.

Agree or remind people of the ground rules

Here is a list of useful rules. People should:

- keep within the agenda;

- speak through the chair and try not to start side discussions;
- try not to interrupt other people;
- try to be polite and respectful;
- sort out their arguments before they speak and be brief and to the point;
- accept the decisions made by the meeting and avoid trying to raise them again in other contexts;
- be prepared to accept a call to order or a call to curtail the discussion on any point;
- share responsibility for time-keeping;
- allow others to have their say;
- listen carefully;
- try to avoid pre-judging or making assumptions;
- keep their own notes;
- accept responsibilities and tasks wherever appropriate.

No doubt other rules will come to mind for meetings you have in your parish.

Manage the agenda

With the sort of preparation listed above managing the agenda should be quite straightforward. Additional points to remember include:

- Introduce each item or issue clearly.
- Be flexible. Time-keeping is important: if an issue becomes more important or urgent than the time allocated to it, make the time and shuffle other items accordingly.
- Summarize the points discussed and agreed at the end of each item and agree the resulting action points along with who should take responsibility for them and the related timings.
- The chair should keep a clear note of all the outcomes and agreements and be able to consult with the minute-taker about these details after the meeting is completed.

Manage discussions

A good chair or leader *should not* do most of the talking. If you want the discussion to be the best possible, no one should dominate what is being said and everyone should feel that their point was heard and considered. How can this be achieved? The following points should help:

- Stay focused on the issues or item being discussed.
- Keep an open mind and listen carefully to what is being said.
- Try to facilitate the discussion with open questions.
- Ask clear and specific questions to help clarify and consolidate important points made by others.
- Invite the group to suggest alternatives, explore and evaluate options. If you have a list, only offer those not mentioned if you think it will add to the discussion.
- Make sure the group recognizes the contributions made by each member and try to build on those.
- Be vigilant and try to ensure that the quiet or timid members of the group have space to express themselves.
- Try to be as open as possible. You do not need to act or feel defensive. Accept criticism and try to build on it rather than dismiss it.
- Do not be afraid to disagree or show your concern about issues but act with care and sensitivity.
- Speak for yourself and encourage others to do the same. Try to prevent people making assumptions about the views of others.
- Try to encourage everyone to share in the responsibility for the success of the meeting.
- Be an advocate for the ground rules by sticking to them yourself.
- Take responsibility for calling people to task when they ignore the rules.
- Seek the advice and support of the members of the meeting and use this to help improve the way the meeting is managed.

With so many different types of formal meeting within a parish it might be tempting to expect that these guidelines are already familiar to many of those involved in participating and running them. The breadth and scope of the guidelines are such that we hope that even the most experienced and battle-scarred members might find something new and useful within the points raised.

Following up the meeting

For less formal meetings, revisit your plans and review how each part was carried through. Seek feedback from helpers and attendees. Be as honest as possible in assessing the meeting's success and seek advice on how it might be improved. If the event was, for you at least, a one-off event, you should still record your experiences, your checklists and plans and make clear notes of how the meeting went, along with the suggestions on how it might be improved. These can then be used by others who have been inspired by your efforts and want to repeat the exercise at some time in the future.

For more formal meetings try this approach.

Review the meeting

Reviewing a meeting should not take longer than a few minutes (ten at the most). The difference it makes can be significant. Try to do the review as soon after the meeting as possible. Look at the list and try it out after your next meeting.

- *How well did the meeting do in meeting its agenda objectives?*
  - Did the meeting complete the agenda and meet its objectives?
  - How good was the preparation?
  - Were the decisions/conclusions/action points good, workable, creative?
- *What can we say about the quality and effectiveness of the meeting itself?*
  - How did the group work together, were issues discussed effectively, were problems dealt with well?
  - How did you handle decision-making, did you keep within the time?

- Was it a good meeting; did it manage to be interesting; was it stimulating; did people enjoy it; did they come away feeling that they had achieved things; did it work; are there training issues to consider here?
- *What were your overall impressions of the meeting?*
  - What worked/didn't work, what was missing, etc.?
  - What are the lessons to be learned and who needs to learn them?
  - Things to do to improve the meeting?
- *OK, so these meetings have been happening for a long time. What other questions should we be asking about them?*
  - Has their remit changed, are there too many or too few meetings, can you reinvigorate the group, would time away help?
  - Have we got all of the right people in this group, are there training and educational issues?

Following up on the meeting

On a personal level, members have a duty to follow up their own part of the work generated by the meeting.

The officers (if any) of the meeting need to carry out their duties, too. The person who agreed to take the minutes should have agreed to type them up and either distribute them or pass them to the appropriate person. This should be done within a few days of the meeting.

The chair should work with the minute-taker to ensure that the details are as accurate and representative of the meeting as possible.

It may be very helpful if the chair or secretary highlighted relevant tasks, commitments, etc. for each of the members in their copy of the draft minutes.

Make certain that there is a process in place for following up the progress on all of the actions in the minutes. The outcomes expected from the meeting need to be checked in time for the preparation of the next meeting.

Ensure that all members have the support and care that they need in order for them to carry out their duties.

Conclusions

Communications are at the heart of parish life. The better the communications, generally speaking, the better is parish life. This is why getting to grips with this area is of importance to all parishioners. One vital aspect of communications takes place in the context of different types of meetings within the parish. In fact, a considerable part of parish life is managed, directed, facilitated and supported by all kinds of meetings. They are also tools for consulting, enabling and sharing within the community.

The more we work towards having better meetings, the closer we will come to achieving our goals as a part of the family of God. For those who never intend to chair or be a key player in a meeting, it is still your responsibility to try to understand what is going on in any meetings you attend or take part in. By understanding the processes within the meeting you will help to make the meeting work better. By understanding what the chair and other members are trying to do, you will make their job much easier. By following the guidelines and sticking to the basic ground rules, you will help the meeting to become a more efficient, effective and satisfying event to be part of.

8
Planning and the Parish: Aiming High

Remember this: Whoever sows sparingly will also reap sparingly, and whoever sows generously will also reap generously.

2 Corinthians 9.6

Introduction

Planning can be a major help in the life of the parish and should be used whenever necessary. Much of what we have learned about planning comes from experience in areas of commerce, industry and people management. This chapter will help you tap in to that experience and put it to good use in all aspects of parish life.

What is planning?

Planning is the way in which we prepare for and map out how we intend to go about achieving our aims and objectives. These aims and objectives can be related to a specific project or event or they can be for a group or even for the parish as a whole.

So planning includes the intentions and the vision of those who wish to carry out the plan as well as the things it intends to bring about and how it intends to make these things happen. It may contain background information so that the plans make sense. It may also include information on how to judge whether the outcome was a success. It should also have a financial element covering costs and income (if any).

In a parish there will be a number of different circumstances where planning will be useful. For example, the parish can have a plan which looks at where the parish currently is and explores why and how it goes about doing the things it does. This plan can identify the overall vision and mission of the parish and show how the parish intends to fulfil these while building on its current situation. Such a plan may identify actions over a period of one year in some detail and over the coming five years in more general terms.

In addition, parishes will have plans for many of its different functions and groups. So there will be plans for the youth club and the Alpha team, plans for the liturgy and music groups and plans for the development and use of the church building and for the church hall. There will also be plans for short-term and 'one-off' projects such as building works or special celebration events. Hopefully, these various plans will fit within and be informed by the parish plan as a whole.

It is difficult to say how parish plans will tend to differ from other kinds of business plans. Perhaps the main difference can be seen in their focus and values. Profit or competitive advantage will not feature so much and what we judge as a success may have little to do with financial gain and everything to do with spiritual, personal and communal growth. We may also see more about service than we do about profit.

What goes into a plan

Plans tend to share some or all of the following characteristics. They should:

- be grounded in and complementary to the parish's vision;
- identify and address all of the key issues;
- be practical and achievable;
- be based on clearly defined and measurable objectives;
- be based on sensible and achievable strategies;
- identify responsibilities and allocate them to specific people or groups;
- be measurable;
- be designed or flexible enough to handle change, failure and success;

- contain a clear set of actions and outcomes;
- map out clearly timings and financial details;
- be easily updated or revised;
- contain a summary of the background to the plan.

Based on this 'shopping list' we can put together the formal structure of a plan. Plans have the following, standard elements:

- Introduction.
- Management summary.
- Background.
- Overview.
- Objectives.
- Strategy.
- Action plan.
- Budget.
- Evaluation procedure.
- Change control procedure.
- Contingency plans.
- Conclusion.
- Appendices and technical data.

The elements you use will be determined by the activities and actions you are planning. So, for developing the business element of running your parish hall, or when you prepare the plans for your parish bookshop, all of these might apply.

Let us look through this list and see if these elements apply to other plans, too.

Introduction

This will contain your statement of who produced the plan, who it was produced for and why. In our case it should set the plan in the context of the parish, its vision and how the planned activity or actions will contribute to the overall aims of the parish and enhance parish life.

Management summary

This summary of the plan can be done as bullet points and should take up less than one page. It is what everyone will use to quickly check on what the plan is, who will carry it out, what it will do, along with the when, where, why and how.

Background

This is more detailed than the introduction and will expand on and explain the different aspects of the plan in the context of the parish and in terms of the action or event's own aims and intentions. It can include analyses, together with a summary of practical issues and problems and an exploration of any external factors which might affect the workings of the plan.

Overview

This is where the points in the management summary are expanded into a detailed set of notes and explanations.

Objectives

Objectives are the outcomes that the plan is designed to achieve. Objectives should be realistic, simple, measurable, achievable, timed and costed. Can you relate them to the aims and objectives and/or vision of the parish, too?

Strategy

This is the approach that you will adopt in order to meet your planned objectives. It can contain more on people, time scales, costs and resource implications, and should cover implications such as the benefits that will come from the planned actions or events.

Action plan

This is where you go into the finer details of each stage of the strategy. It is where you identify who will do what, who will be responsible for what, where and when it will all happen, and how it will all work together.

Budget

How much is all of this going to cost and how will the costs be divided across the planned activity? Unaccounted-for costs can cause problems in the future. Skills and resources given freely today may not be free at a later date. Cost it all in the budget and mark it as donated services, goods, etc. for the accounts.

Evaluation procedure

For the parish, success might be measured in terms of the numbers who attend or who take part. Other measures of success may be the change in people's understanding or a clearly defined spiritual growth in a group or in individuals within the parish. Whatever the definition of success is, look for a simple and practical measure to assess or record it.

Change control procedure

This section is common in plans where different groups of people are responsible for different bits of the plan. If something happens to affect the way the plan is to be carried out, this section will include the procedures for letting other people know about it so that you can co-ordinate the changes effectively.

Contingency plans

Here you want to cater for some of the predictable problems you might face during implementation of the plan. This is where the team can ask, 'What if . . .?' and develop some appropriate solutions to build in to the plan.

Conclusion

This is exactly what it says it is. Many people use the conclusions to simply summarize what went before, but useful conclusions try to look at the implications of your success or failure.

Appendices and technical data

Again, this may not be the most obvious item in most parish plans but it can be extremely useful in a number of different ways. The plans for raising funds to re-roof the church might have appendices which include some of the historical and technical details relating to the new roof. It may also include samples of advertising, leaflets and the results of research carried out prior to the campaign. Alternatively, the plans for a new youth club may include appendices with the rules of conduct for members within the club, the standard procedures for youth club leaders, child protection policy documents, sample forms for membership, registration, parental consent and so on.

Now let us look at the planning process in a bit more detail.

The planning process

Here are the different stages of the planning process as they might apply to the parish.

Identify the need, desired outcome or problem to solve

The plan will start with the parish, or someone within the parish, identifying and defining a need, desire or a problem to be solved. For example, the priest may want to start up a luncheon club for the old people of the parish. Alternatively, research might reveal the need for a youth club or circumstances may dictate the need for repairs to the church roof.

Put together the team

The team may arise from the members of an existing body or committee, may be appointed by the priest or one of those bodies or committees or might be put together as a result of a meeting or by interested parties or individuals coming together to make something happen.

Assess current position

The planning team will probably need to start by collecting information and doing some analysis. The process of developing the plan will help shape the outcome. So, the analysis may produce a better solution than the one first thought of.

Set aims

This is the top-level view of what the team hopes to make happen and will be the basis upon which all of the objectives and plans can be developed and assessed.

Produce objectives

The objectives need to meet the criteria already outlined. One of the popular ways of assessing objectives is to say that should be SMART. That is, they need to be: Specific (clear, simple and to the point); Measurable (against costs and outcomes); Achievable (realistic, possible given the timing and resources involved); Relevant (how do they fit in with the rest of the plan and with the parish?); Time-constrained (how long from start to finish?).

Examine possible solutions

The process of developing the plan may help the team find alternative solutions to the same problem. It is always worth spending some time on choosing the best solution. This process can also provide useful ideas for the contingency plans.

Develop strategies

The objectives tell you what you want to achieve or do and the strategies show you how to do them or reach your objectives. Good strategies avoid complexity, look for simple, reliable options, build on existing success and so on.

Produce plan

The final plan takes each objective and strategy and builds them into a step-by-step process where resources are allocated, people are assigned roles and duties, times are firmed up and prices obtained. The end document becomes the manual upon which the actions are all based.

Act on the plan

It will be up to the team to ensure that what is planned happens. It may be the case that the people who do the planning also do the implementing. However, we may find that some of those who took a prominent role in the planning process step back to allow others to carry out the final plans.

Review and assessment

Do not keep successes or failures secret. The parish can learn from both, so assessments need to be reported and explained.

Now that we have looked at the process in more detail we can see that the most effective way of learning how to put together a plan is to do it yourself (hopefully, with the help and co-operation of others). The following section gives some guidelines on how you might try out the planning process in a few situations.

Putting a plan together

The notes in the following section illustrate the kinds of issues and details you might encounter or wish to address when you start to do your own planning.

Example A looks at the planning of a club, but it could just as easily be for any regular event or project which will have regular meetings and require a number of different types of resources. Example B looks at a one-off or a stand-alone project.

Example A: starting a youth club

What happens when you decide to start up a youth club in the parish?

Establishing the need and exploring possibilities

The parish had once enjoyed a thriving youth club but following the loss of their youth worker the club declined and closed. The young people, their parents and priest were all keen to revive the club, but after a first attempt failed the various parties agreed to get together to discuss the future. The 'meeting' ended up as a series of long discussions where the different parties aired their views and made their hopes and needs known. From the meetings it was finally agreed that the age range of the membership was important (12–16), that the content of the club meetings should not be over-ambitious, that the meetings should take place during term time in the church hall after the Sunday evening service (which was already aimed at young people) and that, wherever possible, the young people would be involved in how the club was organized and run. It was also agreed that the establishment of the youth club could take a year or more to achieve but that no matter how long it took, the team should persist (with the backing of the priest and the parish).

Establishment of the planning team

This consisted of mainly parents, a couple of teenagers who had been committed to the earlier club and some input from the clergy. The early meetings looked at the kinds of activities they could plan and considered issues such as spiritual content, the 'responsible' adult component and legal issues related to these. The new club was not going to get off the ground until the whole of the team had been processed through the police clearance procedure, Criminal Records Bureau (CRB), so they had time to work on their plans more.

Some basic research and preparatory work

The team reviewed the hall and its environs, noting where problems might occur when running the club, discussing issues with the young people who had been members of the earlier youth club, and so on. They contacted their Diocesan Youth Services and sought advice from them. This initiated a dialogue which included the provision of useful guidelines and other materials, some meetings between members of the team and diocesan representatives, invitations to attend workshops run by the diocese and by a religious order in the area, and information about grants for equipment. Useful publications were bought and subscribed to and discussions were begun with the committee who ran the hall to arrange space for the storage of equipment, training on the kitchen, toilet and heating and lighting equipment in the hall. Health and safety information was gathered and discussed. Local facilities for days out were investigated and the way in which the club might be run was looked at in more detail.

Issues for consideration

They had to calculate the optimum number of approved helpers as well as the correct combination of men and women for the job. They had a basic outline of how the club might work and now understood the space so they were able to look at processes and procedures to support the whole project. The issues they had to cover were: membership details (qualifications for membership, permission and so on) and membership fees (if any), forms for membership, length of time for the club, procedures for signing in and signing out, registration, health and safety, food and drink, equipment and games, music and other entertainment, along with permissions and licences (if relevant), noise issues, procedures for dealing with different situations during club time, rules and procedures for the use of the space. It seemed likely that they would need at least one first-aid person present at each session so training and certification was needed in that area, too. They would have to monitor the activities within the club, ensure that the young people were involved in how the club is run and its focus, involve the club in the worship and social life of the parish, build into teams and train and develop the helpers, record incidents and much more. Once the team began to explore the running of the club they realized how potentially complex it was. Their solution was to write it all down. As one member said, 'We will not be doing this for all our lives. Those who take over should be able to build upon, change and update what we have started!'

Start-up ideas

They needed to spend some time thinking about how and when to launch the club. They had the opportunity to obtain some new equipment and present the club's plans to the parish before they launched it. The timing meant that they could start running the club in the winter term, after the Christmas and New Year break. Rather than trying to entice new members in on that date, they put together a Christmas launch party for the club where they could prepare a lot of different activities, provide lots of food and generally present the new club in the best light. Their hope was that this would ensure that the first night would attract a good number of young people.

The plan

With all of their preparations done and their plan written, including appendices showing procedures, forms and other supporting documents, the team presented their work to the Parish Council for final approval and for allocation of a small amount of start-up funds. Their plans were approved and the team moved into action. The Christmas launch party proved to be the correct approach and the club got off to a good start at the beginning of the New Year. Regular meetings of the team allowed them to assess and develop the club as they learned how to run it.

Example B: running a quiz night for charity

Every year the parish selected two charities for the focus of their prayers, fundraising and support during Lent. Parishioners were expected to put together their own projects for fundraising. One group of men who were members of a 'professional men's cell group' that met every week decided to organize a parish quiz night. They gave themselves three months to plan and organize it and their target night was a Saturday evening halfway through Lent.

In order to win the approval of the Parish Council and priest, such a large project needed to be presented as a clearly thought-out project. So, they put together a thorough plan for the evening event.

They split the project into four parts: the promotion, the site, the catering and the entertainment. Two people from the group focused on each area, but they also worked to co-ordinate the event as a whole.

The site

The team decided that the church hall was not big enough for what they had in mind so they checked out all of the available venues and decided upon a local school hall close to the church and containing all of the facilities they needed. Negotiations included access, control, fees, technical details and some staff support on the night.

The catering

They had decided at the beginning to provide a full meal for everyone that evening. Debate had begun with the idea of using a local supplier (the chip shop and the local pizza place were both considered possible). In the end they decided that control and quality would be better guaranteed if they provided the food themselves. They eventually decided to approach other cell groups for help and found a number of volunteers who agreed to provide various items of food in bulk for the evening. This new group also highlighted the issues of laying, decorating and clearing up tables. In the end a detailed plan for how the food would be provided, served and cleared was produced alongside plans for additional decoration and the planning of tables for pre-booked groups, the provision of cups and glasses for those who wished to bring their own wine or beer and for those who wished other refreshments.

The entertainment

They had a basic format for the quiz which allowed each table to work as competing teams. Different sections to the quiz meant that everyone would have the opportunity to show their expertise in at least one area. This required different media but also ensured that the quiz would be more entertaining. To make it work they needed a good sound system, a video projector, a lap-top computer that could be linked into the projector system and a means by which questions, answers and the results of each round could be displayed. All of this had to work in concert with the group planning the site and the other group providing the catering.

The promotion

The team had initially planned for a poster campaign to announce the event, backed up by advertisements in the parish weekly newsletter and monthly magazine. Announcements at services would herald the presence of members of the team selling tickets at the back of church after each service. The decision that tables would be teams ensured that they sold many tickets in batches to groups of people who wanted to sit together as a team. At one point the sales were going so well they added a further row of five tables, giving them another 40 spaces for guests.

The team were able to generate a very healthy sum for the two charities from the night.

In these simple examples we can see that plans do not always end up containing exactly what was envisaged at the start of the planning process. The act of carrying out the preparatory research often causes the planning team to revise and rethink at least some of the details of the original concept.

One of the dangers in having a strong commitment to an idea or concept can be that the team ignores all the things the research is telling them. They go ahead and plan what they want to do and end up with a less than satisfactory outcome. Try to recognize the difference between the vision and the process. Is it more important to realize the vision, or is the process more important?

Conclusions

This chapter set out to explore the way planning can work within the parish. Plans can arise from many different directions and can help facilitate most of the activities in your parish. They are great tools for working out how to make something happen and get it organized, and they can involve a wide range of people with different skills. The planning process can help build up a body of knowledge and understanding within the parish and can help the whole parish grow and renew itself.

Consideration should be given to where parish plans are kept. Perhaps the parish office should have a prominent shelf dedicated to all of its current and successful plans and these could be used as a resource for all.

Perhaps the management summary from key parish projects could be placed on the parish website, or, alternatively, each project should have a place within the parish website where they present themselves and show what they do. People could then see how well they were doing as a group and how they were matching up to their original plans.

9

The Troubled Parish:
Resolving Conflict

If your brother sins against you, go and show him his fault, just between the two of you. If he listens to you, you have won your brother over. But if he will not listen, take one or two others along, so that 'every matter may be established by the testimony of two or three witnesses.' If he refuses to listen to them, tell it to the church; and if he refuses to listen even to the church, treat him as you would a pagan or a tax collector.

Matthew 18.15–17

Introduction

As parishes are human communities they must, inevitably, face human problems, and various forms of conflict will, from time to time, arise. This fact holds no surprises and, as can be seen by the passage above, Jesus anticipated that we would face problems within our Christian communities. We will explore Christ's teaching on this subject as we work through the issues addressed in this chapter.

As with the rest of the book, we will look at types of problem, root causes, the elements that make up a good response and indications on how to develop the most appropriate solution for your particular parish. This book cannot provide definitive answers to legal issues, neither can it be used as a substitute for expert help. It will point you towards such help and appropriate sources when necessary.

As always, hierarchies develop their own responses to problems. These may vary across dioceses and will be different between denominations. If structures and systems are not in place it is up to you, as members of your church as well as your parish, to try to help the powers that be to establish the resources and support that are needed.

Experiencing conflict: key elements

If your parish experiences a situation where conflict has begun to damage the community in some significant way, you will want to identify the key elements that brought about the conflict in the first place. Although some causal circumstances may prove to be very specific or peculiar to a particular parish, it may still be easy enough to identify them as being part of one or more of the following common elements.

Personality

One of the most common starting points in disputes. It can be both surprising and shocking when a clash of personalities occurs but it is more disturbing when the conflict escalates. It can arise from the style and personality of an individual in authority or when a new priest or pastor arrives at the parish. Personality problems or clashes can also be hidden within other types of dispute in the parish. So, even after other issues appear to have been resolved there may be personality issues still standing.

Communications

The lack of, or poor communications can generate a great deal of conflict. Not being informed about activities or decisions can cause problems, as can partial or misleading communications. Information badly conveyed or presented in an inappropriate or insensitive manner may also create conflict and dissatisfaction.

Behaviour

Inappropriate behaviour can be the root cause of many disputes or conflicts. So, dealing with the conflict may only be possible if you deal with the behaviour that caused it.

Historical

Some conflicts are inherited and arise on a comparatively regular basis, occasionally flaring into major conflicts. In some cases it becomes a conflict where no one really addresses the origins of the problem any more. Such problems may require patient research before they are resolved.

Skills and experience

Conflict may arise when someone fails in their role and others feel let down or betrayed. Lack of experience or limited skills on both sides can create feelings that the other party has deliberately caused problems for spiteful or other reasons. Poor experience can also result in poor communications and may cause people to act in ways that are inappropriate or which cause offence.

Authority

There are different ways in which this can be a problem. Inexperience can undermine a person's ability to be accepted in a position of authority. Alternatively, people may feel that they cannot accept a given individual in a position of authority or people may have confused ideas of where particular forms of authority lie. It may even be the case that the person in question truly is not suitable for the position of authority in which they have been placed.

Faith/ideology/liturgy

Conflict may arise over a wide range of issues such as women priests, liturgical practices, choice of rites and music, and so on. Although some may have no immediate resolution, leadership and education can usually help.

Politics

Politics and political actions within a parish are often inappropriate and can detract from the core purposes of the parish. Re-focusing on appropriate and relevant behaviour and principles is needed.

Crisis/disaster

Parishes will encounter a variety of different problems arising from crises, disasters and so on. They can be human-made, natural, from inside or outside the parish. In all cases the cause tends to be both unforeseen and sudden, and the parish will tend to be poorly prepared for it. In addition to all of the natural strains and difficulties created by the event itself and its aftermath there may also be problems arising from criticism within the parish about how the crisis was handled.

Naturally, readers will identify other elements which result in conflicts. The point here is to build up a picture of what causes conflict, not to try to describe every possible situation. There are situations which go beyond these examples in terms of their seriousness. The following section examines these.

Experiencing conflict: extreme situations

This book is not designed to handle specific legal and similar problems where both legislation and the church's response to it are regularly changing. However, there are some basic notes which will help you develop your response to such situations.

The most obvious problems which fit into this category are abuse of children and vulnerable adults, stalking, and all forms of illegal behaviour.

All denominations have a clear and well thought-out policy and structure to deal with issues such as abuse. Any suspected occurrences of such activities need to be immediately handed over to the appropriate officers within the parish and in the diocese. Trained professionals need to be brought in to handle such situations and no one within the parish should try to interfere with the process or adopt responsibilities they have not been given.

Where the parish or diocese has no obvious policy or structure in place, the first step will be determined by the type and severity of the problem. Dealing with the problem requires the help and guidance of professionals from the diocese or from outside sources. In most cases, seeking advice from the diocese will be the first step. Even in the most extreme circumstances this will ensure that the authorities and professionals within the church have knowledge and a good understanding of the situation before bodies such as the social services or the police are brought in. This will help the parish deal with the situation more effectively during and after the due process has taken place.

This applies to situations where major theft or vandalism has occurred just as much as it applies to a case of violence or abuse.

The stages in any typical situation might be as follows:

- Suspected or actual problem discovered.
- Approach authorities within the parish where relevant.
- Possible investigation or discussion at this stage (depending on the problem).
- Approach the relevant department/individuals in the diocese for advice and help.
- Approach external bodies.
- Keep all relevant parties informed.
- Protect the vulnerable, the victims (or suspected victims) and try to direct care where necessary.
- Keep the parish informed wherever relevant and deal with rumours and similar difficulties as appropriate.
- Maintain support and morale where possible within the parish.
- Plan to deal with the expected outcome of the process and possibly invite help from diocese or national church bodies.
- Plan for a period of recovery for the parish and seek professional advice from the resources available.
- Carry out your plans.
- Ensure that all changes and improvements in parish systems are put in place to try to prevent similar problems in future.

- Make the lessons learnt known to the parish as a whole and pass the knowledge and advice on to others through the diocese or other routes.

In a large number of situations it will not be necessary to seek a solution beyond the parish. Whether a given problem requires external help or not, parishes need to develop their own policies and processes to help deal with a range of problems and then ensure that these are kept up to date. It is always much better to have policies and responses and never use them than it is to struggle to deal with major problems from scratch when they arise.

Experiencing conflict: special types of problem

We have already stated that some problems may be beyond the competence and responsibility of the parish. These may include serious forms of behaviour and illegal acts. Typical examples may include:

- abuse;
- stalking;
- bullying;
- harassment (sexual, physical, emotional);
- acts of prejudice;
- theft;
- vandalism;
- drug-taking;
- accessing and use of pornography on parish premises.

Abuse will be something your parish should have clear policy and procedures for. There should be child protection officers or a team who will deal with both the prevention and handling of any cases of abuse in the parish. These people will work closely with all relevant bodies in the interests of the victims and their families.

The other problems on the list above are just some of those that might occur in even the best adjusted parishes. Each of them holds the potential to seriously affect life in the parish. How they affect the parish will be determined by how serious they are, who is perpetrating the problem, and who, if any, are being directly and indirectly affected by the problem.

Even apparently 'secretive' acts such as the last two on the list and acts aimed at single individuals such as bullying, stalking and harassment can end up affecting a wide group of people within the parish and can have knock-on effects with regard to faith, morale and confidence.

A brief inspection of your diocesan website might not reveal the person responsible for dealing with any of these problems and there may not even be an obvious policy or procedure displayed at that level within the website. Anyone interested in developing policies and procedures for these problems at parish level will have to seek out relevant officers within their deanery or diocesan offices who can help.

Remember that even if no one can be easily identified as the responsible person, someone in the diocese will be able to provide advice. If no one is immediately forthcoming, the best approach is to develop a policy and procedures in the parish and then submit them to the diocese for comment. This will initiate a proper response.

Other problems which can arise and which might be better handled if the parish has already developed policies and procedures covering them include:

- crises caused by bad management;
- financial crises;
- organizational crises (loss of key personnel, etc.);
- disasters (natural, physical, etc.).

A general set of policies and procedures may be enough to help the average parish cope with many situations. Such an approach may also help with other types of problems, as listed in the key elements earlier in this chapter.

Experiencing conflict: more everyday situations

Everyday situations are not necessarily easier to cope with or less damaging to communities, but they are usually dealt with locally, without external professional help (unless, of course, they have been allowed to get completely out of control). One of the responses to everyday problems may be to follow the model set out by Christ in Matthew's Gospel, and we will look at how this and other approaches might work.

Let us start with you, the reader of this book. As an individual you have your own world-view, your own experiences, faith and aspirations, your own life and relationships and your own point of view, personality and style of approach to life. What you are as a person illuminates the whole of your life. You are God's creation and are unique.

Your faith informs and guides your actions. Christ's teaching and the word of God are constantly there to help you and you are part of a community striving to realize God's kingdom on earth. As a Christian you understand the commandments to love God and love your neighbour as yourself. Love is at the centre of Christian life, and caring for each other is something all Christians need to consider as they live out their lives together with the rest of their community.

But that does not mean that you always agree with other people or that they will always agree with you, and sometimes this may mean that you will find yourself in conflict with others within your parish. This does not make you less Christian, but how you decide to approach such conflicts may say something about how you live your life as a Christian.

Let us examine the way we approach interactions with other members of the parish and ask the following questions:

- *Do you begin discussions with the aim of having your view heard?* You should be heard, but let other people have their say, too.
- *Do you see other views as competition?* Although competition may not be wrong, it may not be appropriate. Competition is often a test of the strength, not a test of the value or relevance of the views being

presented. When seeking the best for the group, what you want personally may not be best for the group as a whole.

- *Do you diminish or attack other views without giving them full and careful consideration?* Is this the correct approach in parish situations?
- *Do you listen to others?* Humans are pattern-seeking and pattern-making creatures. We look for clues and build on themes. We can listen to the first part of what people say then extrapolate it into a view of what the other person thinks, which is inaccurate. In reality we have stopped listening before they completed their first sentence.
- *Do you interrupt others in discussions?* This can be because you have stopped listening and therefore feel that there is no need for the person to continue speaking or you may be feeling impatient or feel that what they have to say is irrelevant or repetitive.
- *Do you help escalate debate or argument into conflict?* Do you become more aggressive, more assertive, become angry, display signs of arrogance while attempting to assert your view? This can be intimidating and can incite similar behaviour in others.
- *Can you see the relative importance of different subjects up for discussion?* Do you differentiate between those battles that are important to win and those that are not really important? For some, it is also difficult to separate what is important to them personally and what might be important for the group. As a result they can argue with equal vigour for something that is not very important and something that is vital.
- *Do you step back and take time out during discussions?* We often lose perspective through our emotional involvement in a discussion. Without some form of 'time out' we may go beyond what is necessary or useful. We may, as some say, 'lose the plot'.
- *Do you seek to find solutions that meet the needs of others as well as yourself?* There may be a lot more common ground there than is apparent in the debate. Stop and ask what you are both seeking rather than what you disagree about.
- *Do you seek blame while others are seeking resolution?* A lot of arguments lie in the past. If we do not move on, we might stop others from moving on, too.

- *When in a position of power, do you always get your own way?* It is a common assumption that being a leader means that you should always get your own way, that you have failed if you don't, and are being 'undermined' when people disagree with you. However, being the leader does not make you the most knowledgeable person, and it certainly does not make you infallible.
- *Do you ever seek to undermine decisions that have already been agreed?* This may be thoughtlessly and unintentionally done, but it is usually a selfish and destructive form of activity that should be discouraged.

These questions are best asked of ourselves before we seek to ask them of others (which is why we asked readers to consider their own positions). As always, they do not constitute a fully exhaustive list but they help us focus on what we, as Christians and as members of God's family, need to consider when engaging in discussion within our parishes. We need to ask ourselves where love lies within our own behaviour and attitudes. We also need to ask where the care for our fellow human beings lies in what we are doing. If the behaviour we are displaying does not meet with what we know to be the best behaviour that Christ expects from us, how can we reconcile our deeds with our duties?

In some cases we have encountered people who have argued that it was more important to do what God wanted than it was to avoid standing on a few toes. The questions we asked in such situations were, first, how certain were they that what they wanted was what God wanted? Next, we asked how well they managed to share God's wishes with others (especially those whose 'toes they stood on'), and finally we wondered how their method fitted with God's plan. Sometimes, we need to find better ways, more caring and loving ways of doing things before we can say we have truly fulfilled God's wishes. And sometimes the ends do not really justify the means.

On examination, you may find that resolving conflicts on a personal scale may be a useful tool for exploring and developing your faith as well as a good way of keeping your community stable.

As a parish working together there will be times when the way in which people interact becomes critical to the future of part, or even all, of the parish. The following notes on ways in which we can deal with conflict should help.

Responding to conflict: negotiating a little local difficulty

Being a Christian brings with it many benefits. Our perspective allows us to see that our humanity is both a difficulty we have and a blessing we share. The New Testament reveals to us the very human rivalries and debates within the group of disciples around Jesus and it describes the conflicts and debates after the Resurrection as the Church began to grow and develop. We can take comfort in the knowledge that the same process of growth is still taking place today.

Our long tradition also teaches us that while we should always seek to grow as a result of debate and conflict, the solution to any debate may not be easy. Sometimes the solution to conflict will be found in negotiation, and in other cases we will need to accept decisions based on our beliefs, on the authority of the Church or on what is best for our church or parish. Although this may occasionally seem difficult to accept, true authority can provide a stability and assurance that will help us grow in faith and as a community. However, the way in which we are expected to accept authority or the way it is imposed can affect the outcome.

In order to see how all this might work, we need to first look at the ways in which conflict can be managed and then reflect on some examples of this process in practice.

How do we respond to conflict?

We have the passage from Matthew 18.15–20 giving us one way of dealing with problems of conflict. If a person or group is causing difficulty within the parish, the first stage is usually for this problem to be recognized by someone who has responsibility in the area concerned (or for someone to bring it to that person's attention). The problem is then approached at the most basic level. It can begin as an informal enquiry to try to discover what the extent and import of the issue is. This person should try to be as open-minded as possible. It is important to discover more than just the basic facts, so they should spend some time before the meeting trying to decide what sort of questions need answering. For example, how did the problem arise, how has it affected the different parties, is there an underlying problem which has manifested itself in this conflict, is the person or group the real source of the problem, is it really a problem, and so on.

It may be possible to resolve the issue at that first meeting. Spending time with people who have a grievance may be all that is required. Being able to answer key questions and give clear guidance or explanations may also solve the problem. If the problem cannot be resolved it may be necessary to take the discussion to another level. A meeting with the disaffected group and the body responsible for the area under dispute is the next stage. It may be useful to try to approach this through an informal meeting, but this may not be acceptable.

The resulting discussion may result in some form of written statement. From an informal meeting it could be a note outlining the points discussed, their outcome and the items agreed. If it is more formal, minutes should be taken and agreed. More than one meeting may be necessary.

If this stage does not result in satisfactory solutions, it may be necessary to bring in new levels of authority. In some cases this may be an issue dealt with by the Parish Council or the relevant senior officer of the parish, or it may be something for deanery or diocesan involvement.

Time needs to be taken after the dispute has been resolved to work on healing and renewal. There may be a need for time to forgive. You will also need to look at how everyone can learn from the experience.

At each level the objectives of the meeting should be kept as clear as possible. These are:

- *Try to avoid letting any dispute escalate.* Every dispute which is allowed to grow will affect increasingly larger numbers of people.
- *Try to solve the problem quickly but with care and clarity.* If your approach is seen to be unsympathetic or rushed, you will find people resisting even the most reasonable of resolutions. You want to re-

solve things quickly before they escalate, but it is important to show respect, and to help those who are disaffected to move on. Care and clarity are key factors in helping people towards acceptance.

- *Be honest in word and action.* Do not promise anything that cannot be delivered. Try to find the solution that best solves the problem and make sure the solution is understood and agreed.
- *Be sure you understand the implications of the problem and its solution.* Do not agree to a solution which will create further problems for the rest of the parish.
- *Be clear on issues of authority and acceptable practice.* Sometimes (in fact, quite often) disputes will not be solved through negotiation or compromise. Sometimes problems are non-negotiable. If a group decides to try to usurp the authority of the church or tries to operate regardless of rules and laws, compromise is unlikely to be an option.
- *Try to avoid secrecy.* In most cases openness is the best approach. Secrecy can fuel undesirable rumours and speculation. Try to be clear about the differences between confidentiality and secrecy, and act accordingly.
- *Listen.* Problems are unlikely to be solved by anyone who fails to listen carefully and with an open mind.

Responding to conflict: developing responses

How can a parish develop suitable responses? The experience of how churches now deal with the problems of child protection shows us that we need to develop professional policies and procedures, keep them up to date and act on them.

One approach is to put together a group in your parish who are skilled and empowered to develop policies and procedures.

Rather than using a sub-committee made up of the Parish Council members, it may be better to develop and empower a publicly appointed and clearly identified committee and then allow them access to the parish as a whole and provide the parish with access to them as part of the consultation and development process. This group can contain a mixture of lay people and (wherever possible) professionals such as social workers, teachers and police officers. Part of their preparation can be training and team building and may include a weekend retreat where they can work together to reflect on their appointed tasks.

The first task of such a team may be to identify the areas where policies are required. These areas can then be investigated and the Parish Council, priest and other bodies can then be provided with useful information outlining these areas and listing possible policy responses to them. For example, an examination of information on bullying could produce a briefing document and pointers on how bullying is approached and dealt with in other organizations. A policy on bullying can then be drawn up by the appropriate parish body with the help of the team.

Summaries of all policies can be published on the parish website and can be distributed to all parish groups. This will help groups identify and deal with some of the problems at an early stage and provide a clear framework within which all parish groups can work.

The team can then produce general procedures addressing these policies. These can then be used as the basic starting point for resolving disputes, dealing with conflicts and handling problems. These guidelines may follow the general principles described earlier, but the parish team should not be left to work in isolation. Support from the parish is important, but linking into a deanery and possibly diocesan level network of support and professional advice should be both a starting point and the way forward for the team.

Conclusions

This chapter has only been able to briefly explore what is a major issue in the modern parish. The hope is that the experiences of readers will be less traumatic than the situations discussed here. However, when problems do arise we hope that the key points in this chapter will help. Seek to stop problems from escalating, deal with them honestly and lovingly, try to be as open as possible and keep listening. Where compromise is not possible, remember that how you deal with the situation is as important as the actual outcome. Do not try to be an expert or professional – seek good help and advice. Use the professionals both within the parish and in the diocese and community. Keep people informed and avoid all forms of misinformation.

And, of course, pray for God's help and guidance, and keep praying both individually and together as a parish. God's love and support are things that we, in our parishes, can always turn to and rely on.

10

Looking Forward:
Managing the Future

And let us consider how we may spur one another on towards love and good deeds. Let us not give up meeting together, as some are in the habit of doing, but let us encourage one another – and all the more as you see the Day approaching.

Hebrews 10.24–25

Introduction

This book has not been designed as a traditional 'How to do' manual. It aims to be a 'How we can help you help yourselves' book instead. So, when we consider the future and what it might bring, we must conclude that the future is what you make it.

One writer has said, 'The problem with the future is you never know when you have arrived there!' but we will not have that problem.

Those who read and explore this book carefully will end up with two important things that should help them to face the future. First, they will have built a better, much broader picture of their parish and so they will know when things start to change, and understand what those changes are. Second, they will have built a number of ways of working together within the parish and will have the basic tools with which to begin the process of handling whatever the future has to offer.

Of course, if you are to do more than just react to what the future has to offer, there are still things you need to do.

Prepare the way

What should a parish do once it has carried out the kind of self-examination suggested in this book? Should it keep this knowledge to itself or should it use it as a foundation for growth and development? One possibility is for the parish to put together a publication which both tells people about the parish and proclaims where the parish aims to be in the next five years: a document which may look more like a manifesto than a five-year plan.

The booklet could give a clear and positive profile of its parishioners, explain what the parish does and how it does it, and could show what parish life is like, and explain how and why people should become involved in the parish, and reveal the ambitions and aspirations of the parish for the next five years. It could start with the parish's vision and mission, and the inclusive, caring spirit of the parish should be clear on every page. Such a document would certainly be closer to a manifesto than an information booklet and its intention would be to do more than inform. It would be designed to attract and evangelize in one the most positive ways possible – by example.

Putting the parish 'manifesto' together

There are five stages in putting together such a document.

Stage 1: agreeing content

The question is not 'How much?' but 'What do we want to include?' and the answer can be reached either at a public gathering or by a group of people tasked with planning and organizing the document. It needs to have basic information about the parish – facts such as where the church and other buildings are, when services are, who the main contacts for the parish are, etc. This is relatively easy to compile, but the objectives of the publication and its design will dictate where you put this information.

The parish will also have much information about who the parishioners are, what they like and think, and how they go about living their Christian lives. Simple, easy-to-access and interesting pieces of information need to be selected and presented in attractive ways. Include some facts about the history and connections between the parish and the community, too.

Then the team can put together information about why people are part of the parish, what different types of people get out of being parishioners, how parish life has enhanced and lit up people's lives, etc.

The parish vision, its aims or mission statement and personal messages from members of the parish need to be gathered and included.

Stage 2: filling in the gaps

Much of the agreed content will be easy to compile as it will exist in parish records and will have been gathered during research exercises. However, it may be necessary to plan the process for developing the parish aims, vision and other statements. Such statements may already exist, but even if they do, this could be an opportunity to review and improve on them.

A public meeting may not be a useful way to develop such statements. Alternative approaches for doing this have been described in various parts of this book already. Whichever approach is adopted, the more people consulted, the more powerful and representative the statements will be.

We have already described aims in the context of plans. A parish's aims would be broadly similar in definition. Parish aims consist of a short statement or set of statements which encapsulate the primary intentions and aspirations of the parish. The parish should be able to assess all of its actions and activities against its aims.

A parish mission statement is usually an expansion of those aims. It is still brief, but it clarifies and opens up the shorter statement.

A parish vision statement takes the aims and mission of the parish and looks at how the parish will try to live out its aspirations. It will contain a short number of bullet-points showing how the parish intends to meet the aims and realize its mission.

Try to keep the language simple and clear, avoiding jargon and trying to be as unambiguous as possible.

Stage 3: putting the booklet together

It will probably be best to have someone on the team who has put publications together in the past. This is most important if the booklet is being produced 'in house' on the parish computer and printers. If a local printer/publisher is used, the team needs to work closely with them to ensure that the finished document looks as good as possible. Proof reading should be done by several different people but co-ordinated by one person. A good editor is also worth searching for in the parish. A proof copy should be circulated for comments, with further proofing so that silly mistakes are eliminated and sensitive items are checked fully before finally going to print.

Stage 4: distribution

Print enough copies for the whole parish and for distribution in libraries and other public places. Tell the local media about it and share it with other denominations and faiths. Give it to schools, shops and hospitals, and place copies in local offices and other businesses, too. Do not be afraid to be as loud and as public about it as you can. This is a document that says a lot about your parish, and it needs to be seen by as many people as possible.

Have a few people from the parish ready to talk about it when the local media contact the parish office. It is good to have a number of different voices talking about it, in addition to the priest and other 'official' members of the parish.

Stage 5: today the parish, tomorrow the world

Having developed and tested the package, put a version onto the website either as a printable document or in web format. Now you can tell the whole world about your parish.

Conclusions: looking the future in the eye

So much can happen in the next few years. If we are to believe the secular press, we Christians are to expect total decline and disaster. However, the media cannot even get their figures right about Christians in Britain, and they cannot be used as a source of reliable predictions for our future.

The true figure for people who are active Christians in England and Wales is actually closer to 25 per cent and more than two-thirds of the population still identify themselves as being Christian. Furthermore, the population is crying out louder and stronger for help in understanding their own spiritual selves. This is not a recipe for disaster, and should be a clear signal to all Christians that what the world needs now is for our voices to be heard and our message to be seen.

Current problems such as declining numbers of priests and reducing numbers of parishioners do not have to be the basis for our plans or our vision. When churches were growing in other times, the shortage of priests was not seen as a reason for closing down or restricting our Christian activities. People acted positively, with the intention and expectation that things would improve, and they did – it was what they planned for and wanted. With that as our model, should we be planning for a scaled-down church? Can we really build our kingdom on a diminishing and retreating set of foundations?

Useful References

Books

Phil Baguley, *Teams and Team Working*, Hodder Headline, 2003.

James Behrens, *Practical Church Management*, Gracewing, 2005.

John Davis, Peter Millburn, Terry Murphy and Martin Woodhouse, *Successful Team Building: How to Create Teams that Really Work*, Kogan Page, 1992.

John Drane, *Do Christians Know How to Be Spiritual?*, Darton, Longman & Todd, 2005.

Martin Dudley and Virginia Rounding, *Churchwardens: A Survival Guide*, SPCK, 2002.

Michael Eastman and Steve Latham, *Urban Church*, SPCK, 2004.

Eddie Gibbs and Ian Coffey, *Church Next*, Inter-Varsity Press, 2001.

Peter Kaldor *et al.*, *Build My Church*, Open Book Publishers, 1999.

Peter Kaldor, Keith Castle and Robert Dixon, *Connections for Life*, Open Book Publishers, 2002.

John Mallison, *Growing Christians in Small Groups*, Scripture Union, 1989.

Shay and Margaret McConnon, *Resolving Conflict*, Communicators, 2004.

John Pitchford, *An ABC for the PCC*, Continuum, 2004.

Derek S. Pugh and David J. Hickson (eds), *Writers on Organizations*, Penguin, 1996.

Derek S. Pugh (ed.), *Organization Theory*, Penguin, 1997.

Christian Schwarz, *Natural Church Development Handbook*, BCGA, 1999.

Ian Smith, *Meeting Customer Needs*, Butterworth Heinemann, 2003.

P. Smith, *Marketing Communications*, Kogan Page, 1993.
Rosemary Thomson, *Managing People*, Butterworth Heinemann, 2003.
John Wijngaards, *No Women in Holy Orders? The Ancient Women
Deacons*, Canterbury Press, 2002.

Websites

Government

http://www.statistics.gov.uk/census/default.asp

Church based

http://www.caseresources.org.uk/resources/resources_research.htm7
http://www.catholic-ew.org.uk/
http://www.catholic-ew.org.uk/dioc/dioceses.htm
http://www.dabnet.org/pam.htm
http://www.cofe.anglican.org/
http://www.cofe.anglican.org/contact/findus/
http://www.cofe.anglican.org/info/statistics/index.html
http://www.scottishchristian.com/churches/catholic.shtml
http://www.scottishchristian.com/christianlife.shtml
http://www.churchofscotland.org.uk/
http://www.scottishchristian.com/churches/index.shtml
http://www.vatican.va/phome_en.htm
http://www.vatican.va/roman_curia/congregations/cclergy/index.htm

Church life profile

http://www.ncls.org.au/

Across churches

http://www.ctbi.org.uk/
http://www.churches-together.org.uk/

Useful References

Examples of Christian publications, think-tanks and websites

http://www.byfaith.co.uk/paul.htm
http://www.eauk.org/index.html
http://www.faithworks.info/
http://www.ekklesia.co.uk/
http://www.premier.org.uk/
http://www.ship-of-fools.com/
http://www.archbishopofcanterbury.org/index2a.html
http://www.xalt.co.uk/exalt/index.asp
http://www.anglican-mainstream.net//
http://www.christian.org.uk/home.htm
http://catholicdirectory.org/
http://www.shineonline.net/sol2/
http://www.thetablet.co.uk/
http://www.thepastoralreview.org/
http://www.churchtimes.co.uk/
http://www.churchnewspaper.com/
http://www.thirdway.org.uk/index.htm

Index